I0221557

Police Commissioners of Baltimore City

Report of the Police Commissioners of Baltimore City

To the Senate of Maryland

Police Commissioners of Baltimore City

Report of the Police Commissioners of Baltimore City
To the Senate of Maryland

ISBN/EAN: 9783337161590

Printed in Europe, USA, Canada, Australia, Japan

Cover: Foto ©ninafisch / pixelio.de

More available books at **www.hansebooks.com**

To the Senate and House of Delegates of Maryland :

Under ordinary circumstances the report of the Board of Police of the city of Baltimore to your Honorable Body contains a record of their proceedings since their last report. On the present occasion, however, it is different. The last report was made by a Board, two of whose members have been removed from office ; and their successors, appointed on the second day of November last by the Governor, are able to state only what has come within their knowledge since the date of of their appointment. This they now proceed to do, complying, as far as practicable, with the provisions of the Code in this respect. They commence with the commission issued to them on the date aforesaid :

The State of Maryland to James Young, Esq.,
of Baltimore city greeting :

Be it known that, reposing great trust and confidence in your judgment and integrity, and decision of character, you are hereby appointed a Commissioner of the Board of Police of the city of Baltimore, vice Samuel Hindes, heretofore elected to the said office by the joint ballot of the two Houses of the General Assembly, but who has been removed from office by me upon an investigation of charges against him for official misconduct; to do equal right and justice, according to the law of this State, in every case in which you shall act under this commission, and to execute the same office justly, honestly and faithfully, according to law, until the election of your successor, at the next session of the General Assembly, or until you shall be discharged therefrom.

Given under my hand and seal of the State of Maryland at Annapolis, this second day of November, in the year of our Lord one thousand eight hundred and sixty-six.

By the Governor,
THOMAS SWANN.

JOHN M. CARTER, *Secretary of State.*

[The commission of Mr. Valiant was identical in language, merely changing the names.]

It is deemed unnecessary to refer to the circumstances
which induced His Excellency, the Governor, to remove the
late Board. Accompanying his annual message will be found
a detailed statement. The present Board, therefore, confine
their report to the day on which their commission is dated—
not being aware of what had transpired during the period
the office was occupied by their predecessors, except the financial statement, which embraces the whole year.

At two o'clock P. M., on the same day, the new Commissioners qualified before his honor, R. N. Martin, Judge of
the Superior Court, by subscribing the following oath :

"I, James Young, do swear that I will support the Constitution of the United States, and that I will be faithful and
bear true allegiance to the State of Maryland and support
the Constitution and the laws thereof, and that I will to the
best of my skill and judgment, diligently and faithfully without partiality or prejudice, execute the office of Commissioner of the Board of Police of the city of Baltimore, according
to the Constitution and laws of this State, and that since the
adoption of the present Constitution, I have not in any manner violated the provisions thereof in relation to bribery of
voters, or preventing legal or procuring illegal votes to be
given. I do further swear that in any and every appointment
or removal to be by me made to or from the police force created under Article (4) four of the Code of Public Local Laws,
sections 806 to 822, inclusive, and the amendments thereto, I
will in no case and under no pretext, appoint or remove any
policeman or officer of police, or other person under them,
for or on account of the political opinion of such policeman
or officer or other person, or for any cause or reason than the
fitness or unfitness of such person in my best judgment for
the place to which he shall be appointed, or from which he
shall be removed.

I do further solemnly swear that I will support, protect and
defend the Constitution and Government of the United States
against all enemies, whether domestic or foreign, and that I
will bear true faith, allegiance and loyalty to the same, any
ordinance, resolution or law of any State Convention or Legislature to the contrary notwithstanding; and further, that I
do this with a full determination, pledge and purpose, without any mental reservation or evasion whatsoever, so help me
God.

I do further swear that I will to the best of my skill and
judgment, without partiality or prejudice, execute the office
of Commissioner of the Board of Police of the city of Baltimore according to the Constitution and laws of the State, and
that since the fourth day of July, in the year eighteen hundred and fifty-one, I have not in any manner violated the
provisions of the present or of the late Constitution in relation

to the bribery of voters; or preventing legal voters, or procuring illegal votes to be given.

I do further swear that I will bear true allegiance to the United States, and support, protect and defend the Constitution, laws and Government thereof as the supreme law of the land, any law or ordinance of this or any other State to the contrary notwithstanding; that I have never, directly or indirectly, by word, act or deed, given any aid, comfort or encouragement to those in rebellion against the United States, or the lawful authorities thereof, but that I have been truly and loyally on the side of the United States against those in armed rebellion against the United States ; and I do further swear that I will, to the best of my abilities, protect, and defend the Union of the United States, and not allow the same to be broken up and dissolved, or the Government thereof to be destroyed under any circumstances if in my power to prevent it; and that I will, at all times, discountenance and oppose all political combinations having for their object such dissolution or destruction.

Immediately after subscribing the oath, (Mr. Valiant affirming,) the Commissioners proceeded to the office of the late Board, and were informed by Deputy Marshal John Manley, that the Board had adjourned, and that no business could be transacted until the next morning.

The Commissioners then endeavored to have an interview with his honor, John Lee Chapman, Mayor, and after three unsuccessful efforts, published in the papers of the next morning the following card .

ADDRESS TO POLICE.

BOARD OF POLICE, Baltimore, November 2, 1866.

Having been appointed Police Commissioners by his Excellency, Governor Swann, vice Messrs. Samuel Hindes and Nicholas L. Wood, removed, we desire to state that in the prosecution of the duties assigned us we do not design interfering in any respect with the police as now organized, or to remove any person connected with it for his political opinions, provided he does not hereafter render himself amenable to the laws now in force for the government of the police of Baltimore.

We believe the officers and men in the department are disposed to be, what the laws require them to be, *conservators of the peace*, and it is hoped and expected that ;they will cheerfully aid us in preserving the quiet of the city.

We also invoke all good citizens to assist us by their counsel and example, and that they will use their best endeavors to prevent any undue excitement, and that they will also advise all disposed to act otherwise, to quietly and peaceably acquiese in the measures now about being inaugurated by authority of the Governor.

JAMES YOUNG,
WM. THOS. VALIANT.

In order to discharge the duties encumbent upon them as Police Commisioners with the least possible delay, in case the late Board should decline to surrender their office, the Commiesioners rented the premises No. 1 North street until possession could be obtained of the office on Holliday street.

On motion, adjourned until to-morrow morning.

BALTIMORE, November 3, 1866.

The Board met. Present—James Young, Wm. Thos. Valiant.

At ten minutes past ten o'clock the Commissioners presented themselves at the office of the late Board, and upon making known their business to George W. Taylor, the clerk, who appeared at the door on behalf of the late Board, were informed "that any communication that was to be made must be in writing." They retired, and repaired to the office of William Schley, Esq., who sent for Messrs. J. H. B. Latrobe and John M. Frazier, their counsel, when the following paper was prepared by those gentlemen, and the Commissioners again presented themselves at the office of the late Board, and handed the communication, sealed, to Mr. Taylor, who stated that "he was instructed to say an answer would be immediately returned."

To Samuel Hindes and Nicholas L. Wood, late Commissioners of the Board of Police of the City of Baltimore:

GENTLEMEN :

We called yesterday, at about 3 o'clock, P. M., at the office occupied by you, to exhibit to you our commissions as Commissioners of the Board of Police of the city of Baltimore, and the evidence of our due qualifications as such, but were informed that you had adjourned over until this morning. Our object was to take possession of the office, which we supposed that you would promptly surrender. Upon calling this morning at the office, and after communicating to you, through your secretary, our desire to see you personally, we were distinctly informed by him that you declined to admit us to a personal interview, and that you required that any communication to you should be in writing.

This unexpected resistance on your part to the laws has surprised us, and we regret it ; but, unwilling to make any difficulty in regard to the mode of communication, and being, moreover, unwilling to assume the responsibility of the possible result of the course of action which you have thought proper to adopt, we now require and demand the prompt surrender and delivery to us of the office, office furniture, and other things appertaining thereto, the use of the fire alarm and police telegraph of the city, all station houses, watch boxes, arms, accoutrements and other accomodations and things provided by the Mayor and City Council for the use and service of the police thereof.

We further require that you surcease, forthwith, from exercising any of the functions or duties appertaining to the office of Police Commissioners, and that you utterly and entirely abstain from assuming any authority or control over the existing police of said city ; and we warn you, that we are now acting as Commissioners of Police, and that if you act contrary to your duty in the premises, or interfere with us in the execution of our office, you will do so at your peril.

JAMES YOUNG,
WM. THOS. VALIANT,

Office of the Board of Commissioners of Police, }
No. 1 North street.

The Commissioners returned to their office, where they remained engaged in the transaction of official business until about one o'clock, when, not hearing from the late Board, in reply to the communication, they caused to be inserted in the Evening Transcript the following order:

ORDER TO POLICE.

OFFICE OF THE COMMISSIONERS
OF THE BOARD OF POLICE OF BALTIMORE CITY,
No. 1 North street, November 3, 1866.

The Marshal and other officers of the Police of Baltimore city, and all members of the existing police of said city, are hereby strictly ordered and required not to obey any orders that have emanated from the late Board of Police of said city since ten o'clock this morning, or any orders that may emanate from said Board at any time hereafter.

The undersigned have now entered on the performance of their duties as Commissioners of Police, and there is no other authority which can lawfully act as a Board of Police of said city.

Persons interested are required at their peril to obey this order.

JAMES YOUNG,
WM. THOS. VALIANT,
Police Comm'rs.

Shortly afterwards, in consequence of a large number of persons assembling in the neighborhood and around the office, it was deemed advisable to order the Sheriff to summons a *posse comitatus* for protection, and the following order was addressed to him:

To WILLIAM THOMSON, *Sheriff of Baltimore.*

SIR. Whereas, in our judgment it becomes necessary that we should require the authority given to us by the 816th section of the 4th Article of the Code of Public Local Laws, for the preservation of the public peace and quiet in the city of Baltimore:

You are therefore hereby called upon to act under our control for the preservation of the public peace and quiet aforesaid, and you are hereby ordered to summons the *posse comitatus* for that purpose forthwith, to the extent of 100 men from each ward,* good and true men, of the said city, and hold and employ such *posse* subject to our directions, and this shall be your warrant, therefor.

Witness our hand this third day of November, 1866.

JAMES YOUNG,
W. THOS. VALIANT,
Police Commissioners.

Office of the Board of Police ⎱
of the City of Baltimore. ⎰

The Sheriff immediately proceeded to execute the order, when the Commissioners and the Sheriff were arrested on two Bench Warrants issued by the Hon. H. L. Bond, Judge of the Criminal Court, who, after a hearing, ordered the parties to give bail in "five thousand dollars each on the charge of conspiracy." The following order was also issued by the Court:

Ordered—That William T. Valiant and James Young give security in the sum of $20,000 to keep the peace towards the existing Commissioners and all acting under their authority, and towards the liege inhabitants of this city, by desisting from all attempts to act as and exercise the powers of Police Commissioners so long as they shall not have established their claims, by law, to be Police Commissioners for the said city, duly appointed, and the present Commissioners continue in the *de facto* exercise of their office.

The Commissioners declined to give the bail, and were each committed, on two commitments, to Baltimore city Jail, where they remained until the following Thursday.

With the advice of counsel, who acted for them in the premises, they applied to the Hon. James L. Bartol, one of the Judges of the Court of Appeals of Maryland, for writs of habeas corpus respectively. These writs were made returnable on the 5th day of November, Monday, when the Warden, claiming three days in which to make a return, and the Judge sustaining his claim, the further hearing was postponed until Thursday, the 8th of November, when the Warden having produced the Commissioners and Sheriff, proof was offered on both sides, in regard to the return, during that day and even-

---

*This order was subsequently modified, and the number required to be summoned was reduced to one hundred men in all.

ing. [See Appendix]. The arguments of counsel were heard on the 9th and 10th, and on the 13th of November, the Judge gave the following decision, establishing the right of Messrs. Young and Valiant, the Commissioners from the date of the appointment.

THE POLICE COMMISSIONERS AND SHERIFF

Decision in the Habeas Corpus Cases.

OPINION.

In the matter of the application of James Young, Wm. Thomas Valiant and Wm. Thomson, for writ of Habeas Corpus.

Under the Code of Public General Laws jurisdiction and power are conferred on me, as one of the Judges of the Court of Appeals, to grant the writ of habeas corpus—Article forty-three, section one. By the fifteenth section of the same Article, any Judge, whether in court or out of court, who shall refuse the writ to a party entitled is made "liable to the action of the party grieved."

This great writ, "employed for the summary vindication of the right of personal liberty when illegally restrained," is guarranteed to every citizen in the most solemn form under the constitution and laws as a writ of right which no Judge is at liberty to refuse in any case where, by the law, the petitioner is entitled to it.

By the act of 1862, chapter 36, which repealed the third section of article 43 of the code, it was enacted .

"It any person be committed or detained for any crime, or under any color or pretence whatsoever, he, or any one on his behalf, may complain by petition to any one of the courts or judges mentioned in the first section of this article, and said court or judge shall forthwith grant a writ of habeas corpus, directed to the officer or other person in whose custody the party detained shall be, returnable immediately before the said court or judge granting the same; *provided*, the person detained be not committed or detained for treason or felony, plainly expressed in the warrant of commitment, or be not convict or in execution by legal process."

The act then goes on to provide that if the person be detained under color of a warrant of commitment, the petition presented by him shall be accompanied by a copy of the warrant of commitment or detainer, or by an affidavit, that a copy thereof was demanded of the person having him in custody, and the same was neglected or refused to be given.

In these cases the petitions were accompanied with copies of the warrants of commitment, certified by the clerk of the Criminal Court of Baltimore, and the causes of detention not appearing to be within the exceptions in the act of 1862, the writs were issued.

2

They have been returned by the warden, and the petitioners brought before me, with his certificate setting forth the causes of detainer or imprisonment.

These it will be my duty to examine, but before doing so, it is necessary to notice a point suggested by the petitioners' counsel.

Two of the copies of commitments furnished by the clerk, and filed before me with the petitions, were as follows:

CRIMINAL COURT OF BALTIMORE, September term, 1866—State of Maryland vs. William T. Valiant and James Young. Committed in default of bail in $5000 for his appearance to answer.

Warden Baltimore City Jail: Receive into your jail and custody the body of William T. Valliant and James Young.

November 3, 1866, committed on the above.

WILLIAM THOMPSON, *Sheriff of Baltimore City*

True copy—Test: JEHU B. ASKEW, *Clerk.*

And a commitment in the same words of William Thomson, by Samuel Sparklin, coroner.

In these commitments the offenses charged, which the parties were respectively required to answer, are not stated.

With the return of the warden are filed the following, marked in the margin: "Amended commitments, November 5, 1866:"

CRIMINAL COURT OF BALTIMORE, September Term, 1866—State of Maryland vs. William T. Valiant and James Young. Charge of having unlawfully conspired together, and with unknown persons, by force and arms, and with a strong hand to expel, remove and put out Samuel Hindes and Nicholas L. Wood, Police Commissioners of the city of Baltimore, from the office, buildings and property now occupied and possessed by them as such Police Commissioners.

Warden Baltimore City Jail:—Receive into your Jail and custody William T. Valiaut and James Young.

November 2, 1866, committed on the above in default of bail.

WILLIAM THOMPSON. *Sheriff of Baltimore City.*

CRIMINAL COURT OF BALTIMORE CITY, September Term, 1866. State of Maryland vs. William Thompson. Charge of being engaged in an unlawful assembly, rout and riot, together with unknown persons to the number of one hundred or more. In default of bail.

Warden of Baltimore City Jail: Receive into your Jail and custody the body of William Thompson, November 3, 1866. Committed on the above charge.

SAMUEL SPARKLIN, *Coroner.*

The objection is urged on the part of the petitioners that these amended commitments are not properly before me, because it is said a party cannot be committed for one offence and afterwards, without being called to answer, be committed for another and a different offence.

This may be true, but it must be rembered that we are here dealing with the proceedings of a Court of record, and to the records of the Court the Warden refers in verification of the truth of his return. The records have been produced and conform to the return in this particular. If the charges upon which the parties were arrested were stated in the original warrants, respectively, and appear upon the records of the Court, it is not necessary they should be stated in the warrants of commitment.

In 2 Burns' Jus., 604, it is said "that in a commitment by the sessions or other Court of record, the record itself or the memorial thereof, which may at any time be entered of record, is sufficient without any warrant under seal."

Here the first commitment in general words, "in default of bail to appear and answer," must be intended to refer to the offense charged in the original warrant of arrest, and appearing on the records of the Court, and to amend the warrant of commitment afterwards, by truly stating therein the offense charged, is not in any sense committing the party for a new and different offense. This objection to the returns is not sustained, and my duty is to deal with them in the light of the evidence adduced, and to determine whether for any and for what causes alleged, the petitioners are lawfully detained, and to decide whether they are entitled to be discharged with or without bail.

I proceed now to consider the legal effect of the returns, and to decide how far they are conclusive under the laws of Maryland regulating proceedings under these writs. In passing upon this question, it seems to me altogether immaterial to consider what may have been the power of the Court, acting under the writ at the common law, or the power of the Judge under the statute of 31 Charles 2d. Our act of 1809, chapter 125, was in its terms like the statute of Charles, and if I were now governed by the provisions of the act of 1809, many of the authorities cited in argument by the respondents' counsel would be conclusive and binding upon me. But the provisions of the act of 1809 were materially changed by the act of 1813, chapter 175, and by the Code, which last, although not in the identical words, I consider the same in construction and effect as the act of 1813.

Mr. Hurd, in his work on habeas corpus, after stating the various decisions of the English Courts, under the statute of Charles, and the conflict of opinion among the Judges as to its true construction, concludes as the result of the whole . "That in commitments for criminal or supposed criminal matters, the truth of the facts stated in the return, upon which the commitment was founded, could not, either at common law or under the habeas corpus act of 31 Car. 2, be controverted with a view to the absolute discharge of the prisoner." (Page 276.)

An effort was made in 1758 to amend the law by act of Parliament, but was not successful. The author says, (p. 279): "The seeds, however, which had been sown in the discussion upon the bill sprang up and yielded appropriate fruits in American law, long before the passage of the statute of 56 George 3." He then refers to the various State laws on this subject and the decisions of Courts upon them. Maryland is not included in his enumeration, but a reference to the act of 1813 and the Code will show that our State is not behind any in its legislation in favor of personal liberty, and in rendering this writ effectual for the accomplishment of its great end of "liberating the citizen from illegal confinement."

The 12th section of the Code is as follows:

"Any person at whose instance or in whose behalf a writ of habeas corpus has been issued may controvert by himself or his counsel the truth of the return thereto, or may plead any matter by which it may appear that there is not a sufficient cause for his detention or confinement, and the Court or Judge, on the application of the party complaining, or the officer or other party making the return, shall issue process for witnesses or writings, returnable at a time and place to be named in such process, which shall be served and enforced in like manner as similar process from Courts of law is served and enforced; but, before issuing such process, the Court or Judge shall be satisfied, by affidavit or otherwise, of the materiality of such testimony."

Under this law, as under the Pennsylvania statute, which is somewhat similar in its provisions, the Judge will look beyond the commitment in a criminal case, and hear extrinsic evidence, and go into an examination of facts, in order to ascertain whether there is a sufficient legal cause for the detention or confinement.

Such has been the construction of the act of 1813. In Maulsby's case, 13 Md., 637, it was said, with the approbation of the Court of Appeals, "Where a party is committed upon *mesne process*, as upon a charge of crime, it is competent for the Judge, notwitstanding the warrant of commitment set out in the return may be in due form and by a competent officer, to examine testimony and to determine upon the proof exhibited to him the real ground of the accusation, and to bail or discharge the prisoner."

In these cases all errors in pleading have been waived, and the evidence adduced must be considered; not for the purpose of trying the case and deciding upon the guilt or innocence of the parties accused. My office under the writ stops far short of that, and casts upon me only the duty of deciding whether upon the return and the proof there is any probable ground for the accusation, or whether the arrest and detention are " without sufficient cause."

As the charges against these petitioners set forth in the returns are different, and rest upon different proof, I must now consider the cases seperately.

First, as to the charge of conspiracy against Young and Valliant. This has been already fully set out as contained in the warrant which was issued upon oath by a court of competent jurisdiction, and is sufficient in form, charging an indictable offence. There can be no doubt that, without reference to the title of Young and Valiant to the office of police commissioners, and assuming that they were *de jure* entitled to the office, and *de facto* in the exercise of their duties as such, the conspiracy charged in this warrant would be an indictable offence.

A forcible disseizin of Wood and Hindes of the buildings and property held by them, however wrongfully, would be an indictable offence, as tending to a breach of the public peace, and it is settled in the State vs. Buchanan, 5 H. and J. 317, that a conspiracy to do any unlawful act is an indictable offence. On page 355 the Court says, "There is nothing in the objection that to punish a conspiracy when the end is not accomplished would be to punish a mere unexecuted intention. It is not the bare intention that the law punishes, but the *act of conspiring*, which is made a substantial offence by the nature of the object intended to be effected."

Looking to the testimony of Fuller and Ball as to the declarations of Valiant with regard to the intention of himself and Young, taken in connection with the accompanying facts and circumstances, I am of opinion there is probable cause shown for their arrest and detention under this charge, and that it is my duty to hold them to bail to answer the same.

The Criminal Court also had full jurisdiction and authority to hold them to bail to keep the peace in the ordinary and legal form.

It appears, however, from the return before me, that the judge of the Criminal Court passed the following order .

CRIMINAL COURT OF BALTIMORE, September Term, 1863.— *State of Maryland vs. William Thomas Valiant and James Young*—Ordered, That William T. Valiant and James Young give security in the sum of $20,000 to keep the peace towards the existing police commissioners and all acting under their orders, and towards the liege inhabitants of the city, by desisting from all attempts to act as and exercise the powers of police commissioners, so long as they shall not have established their claims by law to be police commissioners for the said city duly appointed, and the present commissioners continue in the *de facto* exercise of their office.

Warden Baltimore City Jail: Receive into your jail and

custody the bodies of William Thomas Valiant and James Young, committed this third day of November, 1866, in default of bail on the above order.

WM. THOMPSON,
Sheriff of Baltimore City.

And this warrant or commitment is set out in the return as legal cause for the detainer of these petitioners.

It is difficult to understand by what authority the Judge of the Criminal Court passed this order. None of the counsel who have appeared in support of the return have suggested any sound or even plausible reason by which the exercise of such power and jurisdiction by that court can be supported. Under the guise of a recognizance to keep the peace, this order is in reality a special injunction restraining these petitioners from exercising a public office till their title is tried and decided by law. Certainly it requires no argument to show that the Criminal Court had no power to pass such an order, or to commit the parties to jail for refusing to comply with it, and that such commitment can furnish no legal cause for their detainer.

In order fully to understand the effect of this order, and the circumstances under which it was passed, it is necessary to advert to the facts disclosed in the evidence before me.

Under the police law of the city of Baltimore, 2d Code, sections 806 to 832, and the amendments thereto by the Act of 1862, chapter 131, Samuel Hindes and Nicholas L. Wood had been elected by the General Assembly, Police Commissioners, and were duly commissioned, qualified and acting as such. By the act of 1862, under which they held their office, it is enacted:

"For official misconduct any of the said Commissioners may be removed by a concurrent vote of the two Houses of the General Assembly, or by the Governor during the recess thereof."

Complaints against Hindes and Wood of official misconduct being made to the Governor, he proceeded, in accordance with the 13th and 14th sections of Article 42 of the Code, and, after hearing the evidence and arguments of counsel on both sides, adjudged and decided that the parties complained against were guilty of official misconduct as charged, and passed his judgment and order removing them from office. A copy thereof, under the great seal of the State, was served upon them, and the Governor thereupon, under his power to fill vacancies in the Board, appointed these petitioners, Young and Valiant, Police Commissioners, the former in the place of Hindes, and the latter in the place of Wood, and commissions were delivered to them on the 2d day of November. On the same day they qualified, by taking the official oaths prescribed by the Constitution and laws. They then proceeded to the office occupied by the Police Commissioners, but failed to find them or to gain admittance. They also failed to gain admittance to the Mayor's office. The next morning the visit was repeated, with the same result—the place being guarded by policemen—and a personal interview refused; whereupon they established an office, and addressed to Messrs. Hindes and Wood the following communication :

To Samuel Hindes and Nicholas L. Wood, late

Commissioners of the Board of Police of Baltimore City :

GENTLEMEN : We called yesterday, at about three o'clock P. M., at the office occupied by you, to exhibit to you our commissions as Commissioners of the Board of Police of Baltimore city, and the evidence of our due qualifications as such, but were informed by your Secretary that you had adjourned over until this morning. Our object was to take possession of the office, which we supposed that you would promptly surrender. Upon calling this morning at the office, and after communicating to you, through your Secretary, our desire to see you personally, we were distinctly informed by him that you declined to admit us to a personal interview, and that you desired that any communication to you should be in writing.

This unexpected resistance on your part to the laws has surprised us, and we regret it; but, unwilling to make any difficulty in regard to the mode of communication, and being, moreover, unwilling to assume the responsibility of the possible result of the course of action which you have thought proper to adopt, we now require and demand the prompt surrender and delivery to us of the office, office furniture, and other things appertaining thereto, the use of the fire alarm and police telegraph of the city, all station houses, watch boxes, arms, accoutrements and other accommodations and things provided by the Mayor and City Council for the use and service of the police thereof.

We further require that you surcease forthwith from exercising any of the functions or duties appertaining to the office of Police Commissioners, and that you utterly and entirely abstain from assuming any authority or control over the existing police of said city; and we warn you that we are now acting as Commissioners of Police, and that if you act contrary to your duty in the premises, or interfere with us in the execution of our office, you will do so at your peril.

JAMES YOUNG,
WM. THOS. VALIANT.

Office of the Board of Commissioners }
of Police, No. 1 North street.   }

Having the evening before issued the following—

ADDRESS TO THE POLICE FORCE.

BOARD OF POLICE, Baltimore, Nov. 22, 1866.

Having been appointed Police Commissioners by his Excellency, Governor Swann, vice Messrs. Samuel Hindes and Nicholas L. Wood, removed, we desire to state that in the prosecution of the duties assigned us, we do not design interfering in any respect with the police force now organized, or to remove any person connected with it for his political opinions, provided he does not hereafter render himself amenable to the laws now in force for the government of the Police of Baltimore.

We believe the officers and men in the department are disposed to be what the laws require them to be, *conservators of the peace,* and it is hoped and expected that they will cheerfully aid us in preserving the quiet of the city.

We also invoke all good citizens to assist us by their counsel and example, and that they will use their best endeavors to prevent any undue excitement, and that they will also advise all disposed to act otherwise to quietly and peaceably acquiesce in the measure now about being inaugurated by authority of the Governor.

JAMES YOUNG,
WM. THOS. VALIANT.

They then proceeded to issue an order to the sheriff, under the 816th section of the Code, directing him to summon a *posse* of one hundred men for the preservation of the peace of the city, when they were arrested under the warrants from the Criminal Court, and Sheriff Thomson, one of the petitioners, was also arrested while executing their orders.

It thus plainly appears that at the time the Criminal Court passed the order in question, Hindes and Wood had been actually removed from the office of Police Commissioners by the act of the Governor, in the exercise of his lawful authority under the law of 1862, and had been notified thereof in the most solemn form, and these commissioners, Young and Valiant, had been duly appointed, commissioned and qualified to fill the vacancies thus created, entitled to exercise the powers and perform the duties of their office.

There cannot be any question of the Governor's power under the law to remove the incumbents if, in his judgment, the complaint of official misconduct has been proved. The law makes his judgment final and conclusive, not subject to appeal or review any more than a similar judgment passed by the General Assembly.

A removal by the Governor during the recess, has the same force and effect as a removal by the General Assembly; their powers under the law are identical, and their decision alike final, conclusive and binding, and entitled to the same obedience. For parties thus removed to hold on with a strong hand, and continue to exercise official power, is to resist the rightful authority of the Governor, and to put the law at defiance.

It has seemed to me necessary to declare my opinion on this question, as involved in the consideration of the order passed by the Criminal Court, a failure to comply with which is now alleged on the return as a ground for detaining these petitioners in prison.

Considering the order was passed without lawful jurisdiction or authority, I cannot remand the parties to prison or hold them to bail under it.

In the case of William Thomson, the Sheriff, the Criminal Court passed the following order:

"CRIMINAL COURT OF BALTIMORE CITY, September Term, 1866.—*State of Maryland vs. William Thomson.*—Ordered, that William Thomson give security in the sum of $20,000 to keep the peace towards the existing Police Commissioners, and all acting under their orders, and towards the liege inhabitants of this city, by desisting from all attempts to act under the authority or in aid of William T. Valiant and James Young, claiming to be Police Commissioners, so long as the said Valiant and Young shall not have established their claims by law to be Police Commissioners for the said city duly appointed, and the present commissioners continue in the de facto exercise of their office."

"*Warden Baltimore City Jail:*—Receive into your jail and custody the body of William Thomson, committed this 3d day of November, 1866, in default of bail, on the above order.

"SAMUEL SPARKLIN, Coroner."

AMENDED COMMITMENT, *November* 5, 1866.—For the same reasons assigned in considering the order passed in the case of Young and Valiant, I am of opinion that this order was passed without rightful power or jurisdiction, and that the commitment under it is not lawful cause for detaining the petitioner.

It appears from the evidence adduced before me that the warrant against the Sheriff for being engaged in an unlawful assembly, rout and riot, &c., upon which he was committed in default of bail, was issued without any oath or affirmation, contrary to the provisions of the 26th Article of the Declaration of Rights, and it being clear from the evidence that the same was not issued upon view, the commitment thereunder

18

is not lawful cause of detainer. [See Conner vs. The Commonwealth, 3 Binney, 38.]

It is due to the Sheriff to say that if the warrant had been regularly issued, I should be compelled to say, from the evidence before me, that the charge is wholly unsupported and without probable cause.

By the 816th section of the police law it is made "the duty of the sheriff, whenever called on for that purpose by the board, to act under their control for the preservation of the public peace and quiet, and if ordered by them to do so, he shall summon the *posse comitatus* for that purpose, and hold and employ such *posse* subject to their direction," and for disobedience he is subject to a penalty of five thousand dollars. The sheriff was bound to decide, at his peril, as to the rightful power and authority of Young and Valiant to issue the order to him, and in my judgment he acted in the discharge of his duty in obeying it; and there being no evidence that in executing the order he was engaged in any riot or unlawful assembly, he cannot be held to answer.

There being no lawful cause shown for the detainer of the petitioner, Thomson, I will sign an order for his discharge.— And will also, under the 11th section of the 43d article of the code, sign an order for the discharge of Young and Valiant, upon their entering into recognizance to appear and answer in the proper court.

After the decision of the Judge had been rendered, and the commissioners had entered into their own recognizance in the sum of five thousand dollars each, on the charge of conspiracy, they were discharged, and at once proceeded to their office, No. 1 North street, when they addressed the following communication to the Mayor:

To the Honorable John Lee Chapman, Mayor of Baltimore.

SIR: Having again entered, and, on this occasion, under judicial sanction upon the performance of our duties as Commissioners of the Board of Police of the city of Baltimore, you are hereby notified that a meeting of the Board will be held at their present office, at No. 1 North street, in said city, this afternoon at five o'clock, at which you are respectfully invited to attend as a member of the Board ex-officio.

Very respectfully,
JAMES YOUNG,
WM. THOS. VALIANT.

Baltimore; November 13, 1866.

The Mayor not appearing at the time named, the following proceedings were had:

Present—James Young, William Thomas Valiant.

On motion, James Young was elected as President.

On motion—

Resolved, That Thomas H. Carmichael, the Marshal of Police, be required to report forthwith to the Board for orders.

The following order was immediately sent to the Marshal:

OFFICE POLICE BOARD, No. 1 North street,
BALTIMORE, November 13, 1866.
To Thomas H. Carmichael, Esq., Marshal:
You are hereby required to report at this office, at six o'clock, P. M., for orders.

JAMES YOUNG, *President*

Resolved, That notice be given to the Register of the city of Baltimore, and to the National Farmers' and Planters' Bank, to pay no moneys to the order of the late Board of Police, or any of the members.

The subjoined notices were accordingly sent to the Register and National Farmers' and Planters' Bank:

OFFICE BOARD OF POLICE,
BALTIMORE, Nov. 13, 1866.
John F. Plummer, Esq., Register of the City of Baltimore:
SIR: You are hereby notified to pay no moneys to the order of the late Board of Police of the city of Baltimore, but to hold such funds as may be at the order of the Board of Police, subject to the order of the present Board.

Respectfully,
JAMES YOUNG, *President.*

OFFICE BOARD OF POLICE,
BALTIMORE, Nov. 13, 1866.
To Cashier of National Farmers' and Planters' Bank of Baltimore:
SIR: You are hereby notified to pay no moneys to the order of the late Police Board of the city of Baltimore, but to hold such funds as may be at the order of the Board of Police, subject to the order of the present Board.

Respectfully,
JAMES YOUNG, *President.*

Resolved, That proceedings be instituted at once to obtain possession of the property and effects of the Board of Police, by mandamus, or such other legal proceedings as counsel may advise, and that Messrs. J. H. B. Latrobe, William Schley, and John M. Frazier, be requested to act for the Board in this behalf.

Resolved, That the notice given by Messrs. Young and Valiant to the late Board of Police, be renewed, and the claim therein made be reiterated.

Resolved, That the order to the Marshal and police force, of Nov. 3, be again published in the daily papers.

The Commissioners continued in the transaction of official business until near six o'clock, when the following was received from the Mayor :

MAYOR'S OFFICE, CITY HALL,

BALTIMORE, Nov. 13, 1866.

Messrs. James Young and Wm. Thos. Valiant :

GENTLEMEN : I shall be pleased to meet you at the Mayor's office at 7 P. M.   Yours respectfully,

JOHN LEE CHAPMAN, *Mayor.*

In answer, the following reply was immediately sent :

OFFICE BOARD OF POLICE, No. 1 North street,

BALTIMORE, Nov. 13, 1866.

Hon. John Lee Chapman, Mayor :

DEAR SIR : Your note of this date is received. We have an official engagement at the hour named by you, but will be pleased to meet you at our office, No. 1 North street, at any time that will best suit your convenience, prior to eight o'clock this P. M.

Respectfully,

JAMES YOUNG, *President.*

The Marshal, on being served with the order to report to the commissioners, intimated that he would attend, and at the appointed time he reported to them. He was officially informed that hereafter both he and the officers and men under him would be required to report to the Board, and to obey all orders issued by it.

The Marshal asked for an hour's time to deliberate.

The accomplishment of the object designed by the Board was an important one. The station houses and property of the Police Commissioners was under control of the Marshal. The decision of Judge Bartol declared the undersigned to be the Police Commissioners, but did not give them possession of the property. To have attempted to conduct the business pertaining to the Police Department in the city of Baltimore without station houses or the necessary property would have been very difficult. The late Board could have held possession until determined by writ of mandamus. This would have embarrassed the Commissioners to a very great extent, for the trial of the writ of mandamus might be delayed, and, by a resort to the Court of Appeals, even for weeks, perhaps months. Houses adapted to the purpose could not be rented, and the peace and quiet of the city and safety of property would have been jeopardized. Thus it will be seen that the object to be attained in granting the indulgence asked for by the Marshal, was important, and the necessity for its being granted must be evident. Upon this single point the efficiency of the new Board depended. Not to have granted the delay would inevitably have caused great confusion. The Commissioners at once saw the dilemma in which they were placed, and accordingly taking into consideration all the circumstances of the case, and in the expectation that at the expiration of the time for deliberation, asked for by the Marshal, he would see the inutility of opposition, the Commissioners agreed to wait to hear from him as requested. The result proved the propriety of the action on the part of the Commissioners.

At the appointed time the Marshal appeared and signified his willingness to report to the Commissioners the next morning, and to them only, and to recognize their authority and none other in the future.

The object so anxiously aimed at was now attained—the possession of the station houses and all the property appertaining to the Police Department was thus put in their possession—the Commissioners prepared to enter efficiently upon the duties of the office; and the late Board was left powerless, with the occupancy only of the office in which it had held its meetings and the books used for recording the proceedings of its ordinary business.

Shortly after the Marshal had retired, Deputy Marshal John S. Manly, accompanied by Capt: W. H. Cassel, reported to the Commissioners, when an order was immediately issued to have the roll of the entire force, officers and men, called at six o'clock the next morning—the earliest practicable time—and he was directed to report to the Commissioners promptly at nine o'clock, those who might refuse or fail to act under this order.

At half-past ten the Commissioners adjourned until nine o'clock the next morning.

BALTIMORE, November 14, 1866.

The Board met at 9 o'clock. Present—James Young, President, Wm. Thos. Valiant.

Immediately after the meeting of the Commissioners, the Deputy Marshall reported that in obedience to the order issued at 10½ o'clock last night, the roll at the several station houses had been called at 6 o'clock this morning, and that the Captains were in waiting to report the result in person. They were introduced, and stated that the entire force, both night and day, except three, had answered.

The Commissioners know they have been censured for not dismissing all of the officers and men immediately after obtaining possession of the office, because they had failed to report when first ordered on the 3d November. Under the circumstances the Commissioners could not have done otherwise than as they did. The law was plain. No man or officer could be removed without a trial. Charges must be preferred for some specific offence, and the offender tried by the Board. In this matter, as in all others appertaining to the office, the Commissioners acted by the advice of counsel, gentlemen who are recognized as being at the head of the profession in this city.

When the order of November 3d, was issued at about one o'clock, and just as the *Evening Transcript*, the only exclusive afternoon paper in the city, was being published, but, before the paper appeared, the Commissioners were arrested; and remained under arrest in prison, or constructively in prison, until the opinion of Judge Bartol was delivered on the Tuesday week following, ten days afterwards. So that, in point of fact, there was no opportunity afforded either the officers or men to report until Wednesday morning at 6 o'clock, the day after the Commissioners had been discharged by the order of Judge Bartol.

Even had this been otherwise, it would hardly have been just to discharge men for not accepting the law as it was understood by the Commissioners, when the matter was in litigation, and before the decision in the habeas corpus had sanctioned the views of the Commissioners with the weight of judicial authority.

There was also another consideration which controlled the Commissioners; the Supplement to the Code, section 42, on page 45, of vol. 1, requires the Police Commissioners to take and subscribe to an oath or affirmation, "that in any and every appointment or removal to be by them made to or from the police force, they will in no case and under no pretext, appoint or remove any policeman or officer of police, or other person under them, for or on account of the political opinion of such policeman, or officer, or other person, or for any other reason than the fitness or unfitness of such person," &c.

Upon inquiry of the Captains of the several stations, it was ascertained that the following officers and men had been discharged in consequence, as was understood, of their failing to adhere to the late Board after the action of the Governor, to wit:

Middle Station.—A. H. Quigley, Thomas E. Whiteford, John S. McCauley, Joseph H. Helm, Jarrett Kidd, John Pearcy, W. A. Cunningham, Aaron Ross, S. C. Morris, Samuel Redgrave, Alfred Morgan.

Eastern Station.—Henry C. Durkee, Thomas Vain, Benj. Graham, Jacob Mainster, George Hoover, Wm. L. Tayman, Wm. G. Mariner.

Western Station.—Jacob Hock.

Southern Station.—Serg. Wm. Gardner, Serg. George F. Short, Serg. Jesse Lippy, Wm. H. Granger, George T. Granger, Wm. L. Sumwalt, John E. Sumwalt, John Taylor, Wm. T. Spies, Thos. P. Penn, John Norfolk.

The Commissioners being in doubt as to their power to remove those who had been appointed in place of the above named parties since November 2, without a charge and trial, deemed it advisable to consult counsel. After which—

On motion the Marshall was ordered to forthwith replace on the force the above named officers and men in the positions they formerly held, and that those who had been appointed since that date be dismissed.

This was accordingly done, and all others removed by the late board, without trial, have been reinstated as fast as vacancies have occurred, and in preference to new applicants, the Commissioners deeming this but justice to those faithful and conscientious officers.

The following note, addressed to the late Board, was transmitted to them.

To Messrs. Sam'l Hindes and Nicholas L. Wood:

GENTLEMEN. The present Board of Police of the city of Balmore beg to call your attention to the note of Messrs. Young and Valiant of the third instant, and to repeat the demand therein made for the property, &c., belonging to the Board of Police of the city of Baltimore, and now in your possession —in the hope that as the demand is now sanctioned by judicial decision, it will not be resisted to the extent of requiring the action of the Courts in the premises.

Very respectfully,
JAMES YOUNG, President.

Baltimore, Nov. 14, 1866.

P. S.—We will be pleased to receive an answer previous to twelve o'clock.

To which the following reply was received a few minutes before twelve o'clock.

OFFICE BOARD OF POLICE,
BALTIMORE, Nov. 14, 1866.

Messrs. James Young and Wm. T. Valiant:

GENTLEMEN : Your favor dated the 13th, making demand for property, &c., asking an answer by twelve o'clock to day, was handed to us at half-past ten ; our counsel are engaged in Court in the trial of a cause, rendering it impossible for us to confer with them until two o'clock P. M.

With no desire to delay unreasonably, or embarrass your action, we wish to see our counsel before responding to the subject matter of your demand. We will send you our decision before four o'clock this afternoon.

Yours, very respectfully,
SAMUEL HINDES,
NICHOLAS L. WOOD.

In answer to which the following was returned by the same messenger:

OFFICE BOARD OF POLICE, No. 1 North st.

BALTIMORE, Nov. 14, 1866.

Messrs. Hindes and Wood:

GENTLEMEN: Yours of this date is received. We will cheerfully wait the desired time as requested.

Respectfully,

JAMES YOUNG, *President.*

After waiting until nearly five o'clock the followi g was received from the late Board:

OFFICE BOARD OF POLICE,

BALTIMORE, Nov. 14, 1866.

Messrs. James Young and Wm. Thos. Valiant:

GENTLEMEN: In the matter of your favor, dated yesterday and received this morning, we have conferred with our counsel and beg leave to reply; that we are advised that nothing which has transpired has changed their opinion with reference to correctness of their advice or our position both in fact and in law.

We are also advised that we have the right to retain our position until the Courts have acted on the question of the legal title to the offices of Commissioners of Police, and to the possession of the muniments of the offices.

At the same time we are advised, that in view of the results of the late elections, the contest in which we might engage, though entirely successful, must be barren of fruits, and might ensure the destruction of the police system and police force which affords security to our citizens and is the boast of our city.

Under these circumstances we deem it due to the public not to obstruct the oparation of the system by occupying the apartments assigned to the Board of Police.

We have some arrangements to make in connection with the relinquishment of books and property, and will, if agreeable to you, meet you at the rooms occupied by us, to-morrow at ten o'clock, A. M.

Yours, very respectfully,

SAMUEL HINDES,

NICHOLAS L. WOOD.

The object sought to be gained by the Commissioners, and which they had so anxiously striven to accomplish, having now been attained, on motion they adjourned until next morning at 9½ o'clock.

BALTIMORE, November 15, 1866.

The Board met.   Present—JAMES YOUNG, President; WM.
THOS. VALIANT.

Promptly at the time named by Messrs. Hindes and Wood
in their note of yesterday evening, the Commissioners proceeded to the office occupied by the late Board, on Holliday
street, and were cordially received by those gentlemen and the
Mayor, who, after some time spent in consultation in regard
to the matters connected with the office, placed in possession
of the Commissioners the funds and assets on hand, amount-
ing to $11,974 48, as per accompanying receipt, after which
Messrs. Hindes and Wood retired.

RECEIPT.

BALTIMORE, November 15, 1866.

Received from Samuel Hindes and Nicholas L. Wood. Police Commissioners, eleven thousand nine hundred and sev-
enty-four dollars and forty-eight cents—four thousand and
four dollars and forty-eight cents belonging to the general
fund, and three hundred and seventy dollars belonging to the
fund for disabled policemen, and seven thousand six hundred
dollars in United States bonds, belonging to the same special
fund.

JAMES YOUNG,
WM. THOS. VALIANT.
Commissioners Board of Police.

Prior to Messrs. Hindes and Wood retiring, they stated
that they were unable at this time to give the Commissioners
a complete list of the articles in the several station-houses,
but would do so at the earliest possible time.

The number of removals from office since the present Commissioners have entered upon their duties has been 62.   Of
these, not one has been removed except in accordance with the
provisions of the acts of Assembly, requiring regular
charges to be preferred, and a trial to be had in each case but
those who had been appointed after the date of their commissions, as by the decision of Judge Bartol such appointments
were illegal.

Recognizing the fact that, among other grounds of complaint against the late Board, was a violation of the law in this
respect, in the removal of members of the force for political
motives, it would have ill become the Commissioners to fall
into the same error.   The power vested in the Board of Police
is great.   It has regard to the peace of the community, without regard to party.   The principles of parties change ; the
principles of good government are unchangeable.   It was the
intention of the Legislature, it it to the true interests of the
community, that the action of the Police Board .should, as

4

far as human nature permits, be assimilated to the latter. If, as individuals, the members of the Board belong to party, in their official characters, they should aim to be, at least, so far above it, as not to violate the plain terms of the law, or to lose in the sympathies of a partizan, the honesty of a judge. At all events in their removals from office, the Commissioners thus far strove to avoid the errors into which their predecessors are alledged to have fallen, and which may have entered into the causes for their removal by the Governor.

The Commissioners have been more explicit in this report than they would otherwise have been from the fact that the matter assumed consideable notoriety at the time, not only in this city and State, but throughout the United States. Many rumors have been circulated as to the powers and authority of the Commissioners, and what they should have done or could have done. A careful analysis of the oath of office cannot but convince the most skeptical that the Commissioners have followed the course the law dictated. They know that it is impossible to satisfy every body. He who attempts to do so must signally fail. The Commissioners, guided by the advice of eminent counsel, have been careful not to violate the law. To do what is right has been their endeavor.

The effect produced by partisan Commissioners of Police and partizan police officers is of two recent an occurrence to be forgotten. A repetition of the events of the past few months is not desirable. The Commissioners in all doubtful cases have consulted counsel, and can point to their official acts as being in accordance with the laws enacted by the Legislature for their guidance. That the law is not perfect in all respects is generally admitted, and it is sincerely to be hoped that you will amend it in such manner as your wisdom may dictate.

On their induction into office the Commissioners determined to make an effort to render the police force more effective. A visit to each of the station houses, and a personal interview with all of the officers and men, was among the first of their official acts, and they are pleased to say that it has had a very salutary effect. The frequent repetition of these visits at the station houses, and to the men while on their beats, both day and night, have tended to make them more faithful and efficient in the discharge of their duties. The consequence is, that the city is more quiet, and there is less breach of the peace than is usual at this season of the year.

This fact is, indeed, as gratifying to the Commissioners as it must be to you, and they flatter themselves that as they become more familiar with the peculiarities of the office important improvements will suggest themselves, which will result in making the Police Department of Baltimore equal, if not superior to any in the United States.

It is hardly necessary that we should inform you of the

great excitement which pervaded the city from the time of our appointment to that in which we took possession of the office and its appurtenances, as the papers of the day made it familiar to the community. We do not wish to attach blame to any for having caused the excitement; our wish being to convince you and the people that our only desire was the promotion of the public good.

As regards the operations of the office for the year, we can only make them from the statistics of our predecessors, except so far as relates to the time since our inauguration.

OFFICERS.

There has been no change in the Chief of the Department during the year.

The force at present consists of three hundred and sixty-five (365) officers and men—an excess of eight (8) on the number when we entered upon office, rendered necessary by report of the captains in order to increase the *inside* night force, so that those calling at the station-house could at any time be supplied with an officer for special service.

This force is divided as follows : One (1) Marshal, one (1) Deputy Marshal, five (5) Detectives, four (4) Captains, eight (8) Lieutenants, twenty-four (24) Sergeants, three hundred and fourteen (314) Men, eight (8 Turnkeys, and is nearly equally divided between the stations, except the middle, the extent and value of property in which demands a larger force.

STATION HOUSES.

By reference to the report of last year, it will be seen that the station-houses now under our control are inadequate, both as regards the comfort of officers and prisoners, to the purpose for which they are intended. New houses ought, in fact, to be built, but we have determined, unless otherwise ordered, to increase the size of both the Southern and Western district station-houses. The latter, although central at the time of its establishment, owing to the rapid growth of the city, is now nearly on the line dividing it from the middle, and we would advise the sale of the lot and the purchase of a new site in some more central locality.

LIQUOR TRAFFIC.

By reference to the statistics accompanying this report, it will be seen that the largest amount of crime and disorder arises from the excessive use of intoxicating drinks. There are more than two thousand places in our city where they can be had, and many where they can be obtained on the Sabbath, notwithstanding the law to the contrary. At least three-fourths of the crimes and misdemeanors committed in our city can be traced to this cause, and we are sorry to be compelled to state that more than a moiety of the cases tried before this board proved from this vice.

JUVENILE CRIMINALS.

There are in our city, as in all large cities, a great many juvenile offenders which are too old to be sent to the House of Refuge, and too young to be placed with old criminals in jail.

We would call your attention to the great necessity for a house of correction, a work-house, or some place of moral improvement, where the young in crime might be placed, and learn some useful employment, and be educated to better things than they now learn on our streets.

Attention is also invited to the subject of providing a suitable place in which to confine juvenile colored persons who are arrested for petty offenses. Many of these are too young to commit to jail, and the magistrates are, in consequence, compelled to discharge them. It is no uncommon occurrence that the same individual is arrested several times. This class of offenders is increasing, and it is respectfully suggested that the subject receive attention.

After mature consideration and consultation with the principal officers of the department, it is deemed advisable to recommend an increase of the detective force, now numbering five men, to double that number.

The Commissioners, upon entering upon the discharge of their duties, deemed it best to open an entire new set of books, and in consequence present to you the financial operations subsequent to their induction into office, with the amount of money and stock received, the amount paid for bills unpaid by their predecessors, and the amount paid by the present Commissioners.

Bills paid by the new Board contracted by the old
Board on general expense account.............. $583 78
Bill paid by the new Board contracted by the old
Board at Marshal's office.................... 168 99

$752 77

The Legislature at its last session increased the pay of the officers and men until April, 1867. The circumstances which led to the increase still continue to exist. The subject is referred to your most favorable consideration.

We would also suggest that the pay of the turnkeys should be the same as the policemen, as they are required to be on duty the same number of hours, and are sometimes required to perform police duties.

You are respectfully referred to the tabular statements of the Marshal and other tables hereto annexed.

Statement A—an account of the receipts and disbursements from January 1st to November 15, 1866, inclusive.

Statement B shows the condition of the special fund of the late Board.

Statement C shows the amount received from the late Board, and how it has been expended.

Statement D shows the condition of the Special Fund received from the late Board, and how it has been diposed of.

Statement E shows the number of arrests for the year 1866.

Statement F shows the number of lodgers and those who have been discharged without trial in the several station houses during the year 1866.

Statement G shows the work of the detective force for the same length of time.

Statement H shows the time lost by sickness and leave of absence during 1866.

Statement I shows the number of officers and policemen in service December 31st, and the manner of their distribution.

JAMES YOUNG, *President.*
WM. THOS. VALIANT.

STATEMENT A.

An account of Receipts and Disbursements of the Board of Police from January 1 to November 15, 1866.

RECEIPTS.	Receipts.	Disbursem'ts.
Balance January 1st, 1866......	$1,939 10	
Finance Committee loan.......	23,865 00	
From Mayor and City Council on requisition of the Board from Janaary 1, 1866, to November 15, 1866............	305,736 35	
DISBURSEMENTS.		
Commissioners' Department. For salaries of Commissioner, Clerk, Messenger, and for office expenses and repairs, &c..		5,177 15
Fees to counsel.................		4,700 00
Marshal's Department. For Salaries of Marshal, Deputy Marshal, Detectives and Clerk.		8,619 25
Eastern District. For pay roll of officers and policemen....................		67,848 12
Middle District. For pay roll of officers and policemen....................		99,926 63
Western District. For pay roll of officers and policemen....................		67,049 80
Southern District. For pay roll of officers and policemen....................		66,254 35
Expense account for repairs of station houses, fuel, light, &c.		4,198 11
Amount carrried forward...	$331,540 45	$323,773 41

31

STATEMENT A—*Continued.*

RECEIPTS.	Receipts.	Disbursem'ts.
Amount brought forward.......	$331,540 45	$323,773 41
Police Magistrates.		
For salaries of Justices at station houses		408 00
Arms and Equipments.		
For badges, numbers and espantoons.....................		480 00
Printing, Stationery, &c.		
For all the departments........		1,295 72
Stock account for horses, &c....		380 00
Interest acc't—discount on note.		574 00
Loaned on account of arms and equipments................		1,962 18
Cash received on account of arms and equipments...........	294 45	
Cash received from special fund.	1,142 8:	
Cash balance paid new Board of Commissioners..............		*4,104 48
Total receipts and disbursements	$332,977 79	382,977 79

RECAPITULATION.

Total receipts.................	$332,977 79	
Disbursements.		
Cost of maintaining force from January 1st to November 15, 1866......................		326,911 13
Loaned on arms and equipments		1,962 18
Cash paid new Board.........		*4,104 48
Total..................	$332,977 79	$332,977 79

*One hundred dollars in excess of receipt, occasioned by an error in calculation.

STATEMENT B.

SPECIAL FUND.

RECEIPTS.	Receipts.	Disbursem'ts.
Eastern District. For fines and costs imposed by Magistrates as per daily reports and fines by board for violation of rules...................	$2,615 70	
Middle District. For fines and costs imposed as above.....................	2,900 00	
Western District. For fines and costs imposed as above	3,505 70	
Southern District. For fines and costs imposed as above	1,854 05	
Interest on U. S. bonds........	232 70	
For Incidental purposes at Eastern District.................		662 40
Middle District................		488 93
Western District..............		741 69
Soutnern District..............		627 69
Marshall's Department........		1,859 80
Fines remitted................		196 85
Meritorious Conduct..........		20·00
Disabled Policemen, sick, and funerals, Eastern District......		1,537 39
Middle District................		1,499 02
Western District..............		651 09
Southern District..............		901 81
Cloth Account.		1,557 39
Paid to new Board.............		370 00
Total.	$11,108 95	$11,108 95
RECAPITULATION. Cash paid new Board..........	370 00	
U. S. Bonds.................	7,600 00	
	$7,970 00	

STATEMENT C.

RECEIPTS.	Receipts.	Disbursem'ts.
Balance from Old Board........	*$4,104 48	
From Mayor and City Council, on requisition from Nov. 15th to Dec. 31st, 1866............	38,930 08	
Commissioners' Department.		
Salaries to Clerk, Messenger, and Office Expenses............		$274 00
Counsel Fees............		1,500 00
Marshal's Department.		
For salaries of Marshal, Deputy Marshal, Detectives and Clerk		1,123 35
Eastern District.		
For pay rolls of Officers and Policemen............		8,395 71
Middle District.		
For pay rolls of Officers and Policemen............		12,142 29
Western District.		
For pay rolls of Officers and Policemen............		8,475 42
Southern District.		
For pay rolls of Officers and Policemen............		8,601 80
For expenses for repairs of Station Houses, Fuel, &c.......		767 16
Arms and Equipmt's, for badges, &c........		50 00
Printing and stationery........		450 33
Loaned Special account........		750 00
Balance in Bank, December 31..		504 52
	$43,034 56	$43,034 56

* One hundred dollars in excess of receipt occasioned by an error in calculation.

5

STATEMENT C.—*Continued.*

RECIEPTS.	Receipts.	Disbursem'ts.
Cost of maintaing Force from Nov. 15 to Dec. 15..........	$41,780 04	
Loaned special fund...........	750 00	
Balance in Bank................	504 52	
	$43,034 56	
Cost of maintaining force of Old Board, 1866...	$326,911 13	
Cost of maintaining Force of New Board Nov. 15 to Dec. 31, 1866	41,780 04	
Cost for the year in full........	$368,691 17	

STATEMENT D.

Special Fund.

RECEIPTS.	Receipts.	Disbursem'ts.
Received from old Commissioners	$370 00	
Interest on U. S. Bonds............	240 00	
For fines and cost imposed by Magistrates, as per daily reports, and fines by Board for violation of rules .		
Eastern District......................	168 00	
Middle District..........-.............	248 85	
Western District...............	212 95	
Southern District....................	109 20	
Received loan from general acc't	750 00	
Disbursement.		
For incidental expense at Eastern District.........................		$70 06
Middle District......................		35 95
Western District....................		81 00
Southern District.		27 54
At Marshal's Department.........		440 78
Fines remitted.................		2 50
Disabled and Sick Policemen.		
Eastern District...................		216 00
Middle District........................		390 85
Western District.....................		107 15
Southern District....................		200 57
Cash Balance on Dec. 31, 1866...		497 56
	$2,099 96	$2,099 96
Recapitulation.		
Cash on hand........................	$497 56	
U. S. Bond......................	7,600 00	
Total......................	$8,097 56	

STATEMENT E.

Annual Report of the number of Arrests made by the Police Department for the year 1856.

MONTH	Assault and battery	Assault with intent to kill	Assault with intent to rape	Assault with intent to rob	Assault on officers	Assault and stabbing	Assault on wives	Arson	Abusing	Abusing family-lies	Abusing horses	Abduction	Breach of ordin'es	Breach of peace	Burglary	Committed to House of Refuge	Comm'd for safe keep'g to Rosine
January	44	8			5	2	19		18	6			108	124		2	
February	62	9			5	1	7		23	1	1		142	147	2	3	1
March	77	5			5	3	10	1	41	2			212	230		8	
April	59	6			1	4	6	2	27		1		212	264	2	6	
May	72	4			4	4	3	1	47	4			211	197		8	
June	89	7			5	3	9		71	3			200	198		9	
July	110	7		1	4		19	2	96	4		1	181	228		14	
August	115	1		3	11		20		94	9			153	218		12	1
September	80	14			5	5	17		71	15			120	237		12	
October	80	16	1		12	5	8	1	32				107	244		7	
November	72	7					11		37				71	257	1	3	
December	86	5		2		1	11		29	2			129	150		6	
Total	946	89	1	6	58	28	134	7	586	46	2	1	1846	2494	5	90	2

STATEMENT E—Continued.

MONTH.	Malicious mischief.	Larceny.	Illegal voting.	Indecent exposure.	Intoxication.	Insulting females.	Interfering with officers.	Inciting to riot.	House breaking.	Gambling on Sunday.	Fighting in the streets.	Fornication and bastardy.	False pretences.	Forgery.	Fraud.	Fast driving.	Disturbing worship.	Desecration of the Sabbath.
January		67			431	1	2			3	5		4			6		
February		73			441		1	2		13	16		3	1		4		2
March	2	55		1	532	13	3		1		9		3		6	14	1	13
April		44		2	544		1		2	4	21	2	5		1	21		6
May		61			577	3	2		1	13	15					38	2	
June		70			688				1		23		2		4	24		12
July		58			718		1	1		3	42		8		4	15	3	3
August		110			706		4		4	5	20		6		3	16		3
September		60			674	1	12				20		3			10		
October	2	56			569		7			4	15	1	11	2	3	9		1
November		83	2		559		5				10	1	6		1	5	1	2
December	1	96	7		508		5		2		15		6	2	6	5		6
Total	5	853	9	3	6947	18	33	3	11	45	211	4	57	5	28	167	7	48

38

STATEMENT E.—*Continued.*

MONTH.	Murder.	Murder, suspicion of.	Peddling without license.	Pickpockets.	Passing counterfeit money.	Rioting.	Rape.	Receiving stolen goods.	Robbery.	Selling liquor on Sunday.	Perjury.	Selling liquor to minors.	Shooting with intent to kill.	Threat to kill.	Threat to assault.	Absconding seamen.	Vending lottery policies.	Vagrants.
January......			1		1		2	5	19	1				8				19
February.....	3	2	1		4		1	3	11	1		1		8				20
March........	2		1		1	5			7	1				8				37
April........	4			3			2	1	16	2				4			4	40
May..........	1			2			1	3	14	2				7	1			30
June.........						6	3		9	1		3	2	6	3			35
July.........				1	1	5	2	1	10	2				3	2		3	33
August.......			2	2		32		5	15	1				6				44
September....		2	1	7		53	4	1	11			3		9				38
October......		1		5					2	1	11	3		10				28
November....	2		1	6	1				3	1	2	2		8		3		24
December.....									19					2				53
Total......	12	5	7	26	8	101	15	19	136	13	13	9	2	79	6	3	7	410

STATEMENT E.—Continued.

MONTH.	Committed in default of bail.	Bailed to keep the peace.	Bailed for trial.	Committed for examination.	Committed for trial.	AGGREGATE.	Held for hearing.	Suspicious characters.	Accused of stealing.	Children's Aid Society.	Accessory to stealing.	Interfering with officers.
January	737	92	32	69	30	960	26	2	7	7	6	2
February	815	116	27	62	30	1050	33		5	2	5	3
March	914	311	38	52	34	1349	31	3	5			1
April	846	394	35	34	30	1339	24	6				1
May	840	406	33	61	28	1368	23	9		1	1	2
June	820	564	48	51	25	1508	31			2		
July	870	590	69	39	48	1616	29	4		4		1
August	788	612	79	97	38	1614	24					4
September	701	632	35	54	32	1454	22			1	6	12
October	684	514	46	43	30	1317	44					7
November	747	414	52	69	44	1326	48				4	5
December	666	401	52	66	21	1202	42	3				5
Total	9428	5046	546	697	390	16,107	377	27	17	17	22	43

STATEMENT F.

The following figures will show the number of lodgers and those discharged without trial in the several station houses during the year 1866:

White Males	11,258	
" Females	1,575	
		12,833
Colored Males	2,187	
" Females	383	
		2,570
	15,403	
		15,403

Respectfully submitted to the Board of Police,

THOS. H. CARMICHAEL, *Marshal.*

Per WM. T. WALLIS, *Clerk.*

STATEMENT G.

POLICE DEPARTMENT, OFFICE OF THE MARSHALL, }
BALTIMORE, January 2, 1867. }

To the Board of Police Commissioners :

GENTLEMEN: I herewith transmit to you an account of work done by the detectives of this department in the year 1866, viz :

Arrests made............................... 242

DISPOSITION OF CASES.

Committed for trial by magistrate.............. 104
Released 75
Delivered to parents........................ 12
Returned to the Rozine..................... 2
Delivered to Maryland Penitentiary.......... 2
Returned to other cities and counties.......... 25
Refused to prosecute....................... 22

Total............................... 242

AMOUNT OF PROPERTY RECOVERED.

Horses valued at.......................$2,355 00
Jewelry   " 2,663 00
Watches   " 4,952 00
Money   " 8,682 60
Goods   " 4,007 00
Clothing   " 2,079 00
Wagons   " 756 00
Hogs   " 930 00
Wool   " 130 00

Total.......................,$26,554 60

All of which have been delivered to the owners.

There was sent to this office and from thence to the Grand Jury one hundred and seven cases of violation of the Sunday law.

Very respectfully yours,
THOS. H. CARMICHAEL, *Marshall.*
Per WM. T. WALLIS, *Clerk.*

STATEMENT H.

LOST TIME, 1866.

	E. D. DAYS.	M. D. DAYS.		W. D. DAYS.	S. D. DAYS.
January......	133	106	January........	32	35
February.....	97	134	February......	15	32
March..........	43	56	March	38	60
April	37	13	April........	7	95
May..........	10	49	May............	42	37
June..........	44	107	June........	16	44
July..........	126	91	July............	16	21
August..........	74	39	August.......	19	15
September......	36	44	September.....	57	43
October	150	102	October.......	31	122
November	113	102	November.....	....	54
December	50	164	December.......	20	79
	913	1007		293	637

The above is a Statement of time lost, by sickness and leave of absence, in the several Districts, making a total of 2,850 days.

Time lost by sickness is paid for from a special fund derived from fines imposed by Magistrates, at the Station houses and from fines imposed by the Board for dereliction of duties. Members of the Police who have contracted sickness or been disabled while in the discharge of their duty, are paid their salary in full for twelve months, after being placed on the disabled list, as provided by law—Sec. 813, Article 4, page 316—Code, vol. 11.

STATEMENT I.

Permanent Police Force of the City of Baltimore, December 31st, 1866.

Board of Police.

JAMES YOUNG, *President.*

WILLIAM T. VALIANT.

Ex-officio, Hon. JOHN LEE CHAPMAN, *Mayor of the City.*

Secretary to the Board.

GEO. W. TAYLOR.

Marshal.

THOS. H. CARMICHAEL.

Deputy Marshal.

JOHN S. MANLY.

Clerk at Marshal's Office.

JOHN L. THOMAS, SR.

Recapitulation.

Marshal	1	
Deputy Marshall	1	
Captains	4	
Lieutenants	8	
Sergeants	24	
Turnkeys	8	
Total number of officers		46

Policemen—

Eastern District	70	
Middle "	106	
Western "	69	
Southern "	69	
Total number of Policemen		314
Detective officers		5
Total number of force		365

CHANGES IN THE FORCE DURING 1866.

Resignations to the old Board...................... 36
Refused to perform duty................... 31
Deaths.................................. 5
Dismissed for violating rules..................... 12
                                               — 84
Resignations to new Board....................... 6
Dismissed for violating rules and other causes....... 56
                                               — 62

APPENDIX.

That there may be a continuous history of circumstances attending this case, it has been deemed advisable to publish the whole proceedings before the Courts, that it may be bound with the report published by the Governor.

WRIT OF HABEAS CORPUS.

At 8½ o'clock on Saturday night, after the Commissioners and Sheriff had been committed to jail, application was made to Hon. James L. Bartol, associate Judge of the Court of Appeals, at his residence in this city, for writs of habeas corpus, addressed to Thomas C. James, Esq., Warden of the city jail, to produce before him the bodies of Messrs. Young and Valiant, the newly appointed Commissioners of Police, and Mr. ˻Thomson, the Sheriff of Baltimore city, at the room of the Circuit Court of Baltimore, at 9 o'clock on Monday morning, November 5, 1866, with the cause of their detention, &c. Judge Bartol granted three separate writs, the two for the release of the Police Commissioners, on the petition of their counsel, Messrs. Latrobe, Schley and Frazier, and the writ for the release of the Sheriff, was on the petition of his own counsel, Orville Horwitz, Esq.

The writs were served on the Warden on Monday morning, between 7 and 8 o'clock.

[From the Baltimore Sun.]

FAILURE OF THE WARDEN.

Judge Bartol was punctually upon the bench.

Mr. Latrobe said: The writs were served this morning, between seven and eight o'clock, in ample time for the Warden of the Jail to produce the three prisoners in Court. A gentleman of the bar, (Mr. Whitney,) has just told us—now past nine o'clock—that the Warden of the Jail was here, but without the prisoners ; that he had exhausted, if I understood his language correctly, all his means of conveyance, and had come to the Court house for the purpose of procuring other means of bringing the prisoners forth. It did recur to me at the time this statement was made, that the nearest hack stand would have been a more appropriate place to search for a conveyance than the Circuit Court room of the city of Baltimore. Whether this is but a part of the system of delays and procrastinations resorted to by the other side, it does not become me to say, and I do not say. The result is that we are here awaiting the Warden's obedience to the Court.

Judge Bartol said: I think there is a provision in the code allowing the Warden, in such cases, a certain time within which he may appear and respond to the writ. I do not remember precisely the provisions, but I think it allows the Warden three days for the service of the writ.

Mr. Schley said: Three days is the time limited, except in cases of distant residences. I would suggest that under the common law the party is bound to respond immediately to the writ. I think preference ought to be given to this great writ of right over all mere criminal cases.

Judge Bartol said: The writs were issued on Saturday afternoon, at about five o'clock, I think. It was my expectation that the writs would have been served that evening. It seems that they were not served until this morning, and the delay which has occurred is not unnatural.

Mr. Schley said; I think it would be better to wait a reasonable time.

After waiting until about half-past ten o'clock, Mr. Horwith said: We have waited nearly one hour and a half upon the Warden to bring in the prisoners in his charge, under the exigency of the writ issued by your Honor. I don't think, under the circumstances, that there is any probability that he designs to comply with the requirements of the writ. The law, fortunately, has provided a remedy in a case of that kind. I ask your Honor's attention ·for a moment while I read a petition I have here prepared, under the habeas corpus act.

Mr. Alexander here appeared in Court.

Mr. Horwitz continued: Seeing my learned brother appear in Court (Mr. Alexander) I inquired whether those parties were to be brought in, and he says he don't know.

Mr. Alexander said: I will state that I had understood Mr. James, the Warden of the Jail, was in consultation with his counsel, and that some time would be required to prepare a return, but that is a mere understanding of mine, to which I cannot pledge myself.

Mr. Horwitz said: I have heard from Mr. James, and his answer is that he is in a bad way, between two fires.

Mr. Horwitz having read the law above referred to said: Your Honor will observe that by the 4th section of the same article, the writ of *habeas corpus* is directed to the party having the persons in custody, and is served either by leaving it with him or at the place of incarceration. In this section the law is modified so that in the event of the parties not obeying the writ, or attempting to evade it, it then becomes the duty of the sheriff, under the direction of the Court, and by the authority of the clause inserted in the writ, to serve the writ and to bring the party in contumacy, together with the persons in his charge, before the court.

Judge Bartol requested Mr. H. to read the other sections of the law on the subject; after which

Mr. Horwitz, said: In no case shall there be a delay beyond three days in making the return of the writ, unless the party is more than twenty miles beyond the jurisdiction of the Court. That is provided for by the 5th section.

But if there is no reason why the party should not be brought in, in accordance with the exigency of the writ, he is then to bring, him here according to the command of the writ ; but that under no circumstances shall the delay be beyond three days from the service of the writ. But if there be no such reasons—if the prisoners can be had without any trouble, and can be brought before the Court immediately— then, according to the command of the writ, they are to be produced before the Court. The pretence here is, and the only pretence why the prisoners were not produced at the hour named here, was, that the Warden had no means of conveyance; that he had exhausted them in bringing some thirty odd prisoners to another Court, which did not convene until an hour after the time named in the writ.

In accordance with the sixth section, we have prepared a petition, signed on behalf of Sheriff Thompson by his counsel, stating the fact of the service of the writs, &c., and further showing that the petitioner has probable cause for believing that the said warden designs to evade, and is now attempting to evade, the execution of said writ. Wherefore he prays your Honor to insert in said writ a clause commanding the Sheriff of Baltimore city to serve the writ aforesaid on the said warden, and to cause him immediately to appear before your Honor, together with the said William Thomson.

Judge Bartol asked what proof he had that the writ had been served, and, upon being shown it, he said, "This is a mere memorandum from the Sheriff's officer that he served the writ. The writ is not returned. Mr. Alexander, whom do you represent?

Mr. Alexander.—I represent the Commissioners, who have a deep interest in the preservation of the peace of the city, and in seeing that this case is carefully heard and disposed of. I appear at the instance, also, of the State's Attorney, to render him such assistance as I am able in the discussion of this matter. I would, therefore, represent, the warden, of course. I wish to say that I have reason to believe that the warden is yet in consultation with his counsel, and is preparing or about to prepare his return.

Mr. Schley.—What will that return be?

Mr. Alexander.—I don't know.

Mr. Schley.—You are his counsel.

Mr. Alexander.—I am counsel here, Having advised the arrest of these parties as counsel, I do not care to put myself in the relation of counsel and client with the warden, and will confine my labors, therefore, to the discussion of any questions which may be present before this court, and all other proceedings before your Honor in this matter. I was about to say, though speculating only upon what I have heard, that the parties will be produced in court somewhere about midday, after the return has been prepared. But I make no pledges upon that subject whatever. But I am inclined to think that by mid-day there will be no necessity for any further proceedings at all, but that is mere speculation upon my part. I would, therefore, suggest to your Honor that, looking to the quiet and order of the city, there is no purpose to be subserved by any immediate proceedings of any kind. On the contrary, I would state, as a gentleman to gentlemen, that your Honor will, perhaps, best promote every object of this proceeding by postponing the matter before you until the hour of 12 or 1 o'clock.

Mr. Schley.—I appear on behalf of the Commissioners appointed by Governor Swann. In their case there is no difficulty about issuing any order directed through the Sheriff, because they are not one and the same person. But now, you see the time is delayed, of which you will judicially take notice, one hour and a half, and that you, the representative of the sovereignty of the State, upon the application of the citizens of the State, in a matter concerning their civil liberty, have waited patiently for a return from the warden of any kind or description of the writ you have issued. There is no liberty in a land where a party restrained of his liberty is not to be heard in some court of justice. I mean to speak as plainly and as quietly as I can, although my bosom is full of warm and indignant feeling. Here is a man who has in his custody three or four fellow-citizens, and he has not deigned to make any return, but sends counsel here, who say they are ready to argue any question of the law, but who don,t know anything about the return. Why have we not an answer? The warden is here in the court-house, and has been an hour and a half. He has made no return whatever to that writ. Are we to sit here, hour after hour, upon the faith of counsel that he verily believes it will be so and so, and yet tells us he has no definite information, or that something may occur outside that will render any further proceedings unnecessary.

Could we have any assurance upon which we can rely, we would be willing to wait a reasonable time. We have a right to know upon what he founds his suggestions. But it is staying the hand of the law. We shall prepare our affidavits in the case of the Commissioners and ask your Honor to compel the immediate attendance of the warden with his prisoners.

Alexander Rogers, Esq., deputy State's attorney, said; The only question in this case is, is the warden *in delicto* for non-return of the writ. There is no return of the writ. There is not a legal presumption th t the men are in his custody, nor has there been any delinquency. Mr. Rogers justified the warden in delaying his return, and suggested that the proper course would be to wait for it.

Mr. Schley.—If the counsel knows that a return will be made, he ought to know what the return will be.

Mr. Rogers.—I do not know what the return will be.

Mr. Schley.—Then I shall persist in my application, and will prepare the affidavits, &c., for a writ to compel the presence of the warden and those in his custody.

Mr. Schley then occupied considerable length of time in the preparation of the necessary papers, setting forth the facts in the case &c., which were sworn to in court before Wm. H. Hayward, Esq.

Before presenting the papers Mr. Schley inquired of Mr. Alexander what assurance he could give that a satisfactory adjustment of the difficulty was being made?

Mr. Alexander.—I will say now, what I said before, that an arrangement will be made that is satisfactory, but further I say nothing.

Mr. Schley.—The first motion that I have to make is that your Honor issue an order to the deputy sheriff.to produce the warden and all the parties immediately in court. Mr. James is evading the writ. Has he a right to take the ground that he will, upon his own motion, keep in custody three citizens without any reason assigned, and for some purpose not assigned? He has been within the walls of the court-house within the hour. Is this not contempt of your Honor? Is it not contumacy? What right has he to take outside counsel without consulting your Honor? He has a motive, for it is known to everybody. Three important persons are stayed in their action, and are kept in prison for the purpose of preventing their action. The law would protect him if he obeyed the law. But is he not in sympathy with others? Mr. Schley next discussed the acts of Assembly relating to the subject, and said: In this case the order of the Governor disrobes the old commissioners of all official authority, and they are now acting without authority. But we cannot act upon these matters until the parties are produced.

7

Mr. Alexander said he thought his suggestion would be satisfactory. We have said nothing to delay—we played no cards for delay.

Mr. Latrobe.—Yes, you have thrown a whole pack of cards in our faces.

Mr. Alexander.—If there is any proposition to be discussed let us know it.

Mr. Latrobe,—May it please your Honor. there is evidence enough before you in the passage of time to justify us in asking an order to bring into court the parties. The warden is, perhaps, within the sound of my voice, exulting, with others, in the euchre which has been so successfully played.

The subject of the order and the legality of amending proceedings in a case of habeas corpus was further discussed by Mr. Alexander, Mr. Rogers, Mr. R. Stocket Mathews, (counsel for Mr. James,) Mr. Horwitz, Mr. Latrobe, and Mr. Schley, at great length, the entire argument occupying several hours. Upon its conclusion, at 2½ P. M., Judge Bartol decided that he had no power under the law to compel the warden, Mr. James, to make a return to the writs of habeas corpus within less than three days from the time of their service, which would be on Thursday morning at 9 o'clock. He then postponed the further hearing of the case until that time.

THE WARDEN MAKES A RETURN.

Thursday Morning, November 8.

Judge Bartol appeared in the Circuit Court room at 9 o'clock, as also the counsel for the petitioners, Messrs. Schley, Latrobe, Frazier and Horwitz, and Messrs. Stockbridge. Stirling, Mathews, Alexander, the State Attorney Mr. Maund, and his deputy, Mr. Alexander Rogers, for the respondent. Precisely at 9 o'clock, the warden of the jail, Thomas C. James, appeared with Messrs Thomson, Valiant and Young, who were warmly greeted by their friends. The court room soon become so uncomfortably crowded with spectators that application was made to Judge Martin, of the Superior Court, for the use of his court-room, which was cheerfully accorded, and the hearing, at 10 o'clock, was adjourned to the large room of the Superior Court.

Considerable time was occupied by counsel in the preparation of papers, and it was not until 11 o'clock that Mr. Rogers, of counsel for the warden of the jail, (Mr. James,) rose to read the returns to the writs of habeas corpus, as follows:

THE WARDEN'S RETURN.

To the Honorable James L. Bartol, Judge of the Court of Appeals of Maryland :

The undersigned, the warden of Baltimore city jail, in compliance with the command of the writ of habeas corpus hereto annexed, by way of return thereof respectfully states that he now produces before your honor the body of James Young ; and your respondent, for cause of the capture and detention of the said James Young, assigns as follows :

That on Saturday, the 3rd day of November, A. D. 1866, the said James Young was arrested in pursuance of a writ issued from the Criminal Court of Baltimore, which said writ or warrant of arrest, sealed with the seal of the said court, is according to the tenor following :

[Here the warrant was recited.]

And being brought before the said court, in pursuance of the aforegoing warrant of arrest, was, therefore, on the day and year aforesaid, in default of bail, committed by the said court to the custody of your respondent for and on account of causes which, by the records of the said court, will fully appear.

And your respondent further says that he did, on the 3d day of November, in the year aforesaid, at the city aforesaid, receive the body of the said James Young, from one William Thomson, who was then and there sheriff for the city of Baltimore, under and by virtue of two warrants of commitment, issued by the Criminal Court of Baltimore, copies of which said warrants are hereunto annexed and prayed to be made a part of this return. And your respondent further says that he now doth hold and detain the said James Young under and by virtue of the aforesaid warrants of the commitment, issued in like manner by the said Criminal Court of Baltimore, copies of which other two warrants of commitment are hereunto annexed and prayed to be made a part of this return.

All of which is herewith respectfully submitted to your Honor's judgment.

THOMAS C. JAMES.

The warrants referred to above are as follows :

The first commitment dated November 3, is in default of $5,000 bail for appearance to answer.

The second commitment, dated November 3, is as follows : "By the Criminal Court of Baltimore. Ordered, that Wm. T. Valiant and James Young give security in the sum of $20,000, to keep the peace towards the existing police commissioners, and all acting under their orders, and towards the liege inhabitants of this city, by desisting from all attempts to act as and exercise the powers of the police commissioners, so long as they shall not have established their claims by law to be police commissioners for the said city, duly appointed, and the present commissioners continue in the *de facto* exercise of their office."

The third and amended commitment is dated November 5th, and charges William Thomas Valiant and James Young, with having unlawfully conspired together with unknown persons, by force and arms, and with the strong hand, to expel, remove and put out Samuel Hindes and Nicholas L. Wood, police commissioners of the city of Baltimore, from the offices, building and property now occupied and possessed by them as such police commissioners.

The return in each of the three cases was similar, except that the warrant against the Sheriff charged that he was engaged in an unlawful assembly, rout and riot, with certain persons unknown, to the number of one hundred or more.

Mr. Schley said that the amended warrant, dated November 5, was issued under what system of proceedings and what practice he is unable to say. He will not attempt to explain the probable motives, in view of the circumstances:

ANSWER TO THE RETURN.

Mr. Latrobe then read the answer of the counsel for petitioners as follows :

In the matter of the application of James Young for a writ of habeas corpus, before the Hon. James L. Bartol, Judge of the Court of Appeals of Maryland.

The petitioner in the above cause, by his attorneys, comes here into court, and as to the return made by Thos. C. James, the warden of the jail of Baltimore city, to the writ of habeas corpus heretofore issued, requiring the said warden to produce the body of the petitioner before the judge issuing the same, without admitting the truth of said return, says that there is not, from anything apparent on the face of said return, and the exhibits therewith, or in the facts of this case, sufficient legal cause for the detention and confinement of the petitioner by the said defendant, the warden aforesaid, inasmuch as the petitioner alleges and is ready to prove that he, the petitioner, together with Wm. Thomas. Valiant, were duly appointed commissioners of the Board of Police of the city of Baltimore, under the great seal of the State, dated on the 2d of November, 1866, and that, having qualified under the said commission, accordingly, the petitioner, and the said Wm. T. Valiant became entitled to exercise and perform the duties appertaining to the said office, in the city of Baltimore, without the let or hindrance of any person whatever, and without being obliged to resort to any legal tribunal to establish the validity of the said appointment, or to authorize the petitioner and the said William T. Valiant to proceed forthwith, after they had duly qualified according to law, to discharge its functions, and the petitioner further, by way of plea, says that the order of the Criminal Court of Baltimore city, in the following words, [the order of Judge Bond directing the commitment was here recited] was altogether, unauthorized and passed without regard to the rights of the petitioner and the said Wm. T. Valiant, inasmuch as it assumed that the im-

mediate predecessors of the petitioner and the said Wm. T.
Valiant, in the office of commissioners of the Board of Police,
were entitled to exercise their functions as such until your
petitioner and the said Wm. T. Valiant should have established their right to the office otherwise than by the produc-
tion of their commissions aforesaid, and proof of their qualification.

And inasmuch as your petitioner was held upon a commitment issued under the above order, in consequence of his refusal to give the security therein required, he prays that he
may be discharged from confinement by the order of this honorable court to be passed in the premises.

And the petitioner, to so much of the said return as sets
out the warrants charging him with riot or inciting a riot in
the said city, answers and says that they do not, nor do either
of them, afford sufficient ground for his detention by the defendant.

The answer in the case of Wm. T. Valiant is the same as
the above, and further, as to said warrants, the petitioner
says, by way of plea, that he was not, in point of fact, engaged in a riot or riots, or inciting the same, as charged in
said warrant.

Mr. Latrobe said that under the law they may controvert
the truth of the returns, and plead there is not sufficient
cause for detention, and also offer any matter by which it
shall appear that there is not such legal cause.

Mr. Horwitz, counsel for Sheriff Thomson, read his answer
to the return, modified to suit the circumstances of his case,
denying that he was engaged in any unlawful assembly, riot
or rout; alleging that Messrs. Young and Valiant had been
legally appointed police commissioners, and that the Sheriff
was bound to obey their orders, and that the commitments do
not present a sufficient legal cause for his detention. Mr.
Horwitz said the Sheriff stood in a peculiar position; if he
refused to obey the police commissioners, he was liable, under
the law, in a penalty of $5,000. He also said that for the
present the pleadings are made up.

Mr. Rogers, for respondents, said the answers to our returns
are of a very ambiguous character. The counsel have not
traversed the return nor taken exception to the facts of the
case. We find it necessary only to reassert the sufficiency of
our return.

Mr. Schley.—We are willing to meet you on that issue.

A COMPROMISE PROPOSED.

At this stage of the proceedings the counsel for the old
commissioners privately submitted the following proposal of
compromise. The knowledge of this proposal and the
response was confined to the counsel in the case.

All further proceedings under the writs of habeas corpus to

be abandoned ; the State's Attorney to waive his application for surety to keep the peace ; the parties to be discharged on their personal recognizance, and on nominal bonds to answer the charge of riot, &c. ; the new commissioners to proceed by mandamus to assert their title, and, until a determination of the questions of title, they are not to resort to force against the old commissioners, or to any other proceeding which may not be advised as necessary to complete their right to sue out a mandamus.

No question of title to be prejudiced by this arrangement, the sole object of the parties being to avoid the necessity or possibility of a collision by force until the great question of title shall be conclusively determined.

THE PROPOSAL DECLINED.

In answer to the suggestions, the petitioners' counsel stated :

1. That it remains for the counsel of the warden, and the State's Attorney, and for Messrs. Hindes and Wood, late commissioners, to adopt such action in reference to the police commissioners, (Messrs. Young and Valiant,) and in reference to Sheriff Thomson, as they may think proper, and as most likely to preserve the peace of the city. If the demand of a recognizance in the penalty of $20,000 to be given by the police commissioners (Messrs Young and Valiant) and by the Sheriff be abandoned, we shall be pleased to see such action on the part of counsel on the other side ; but it must be their spontaneous act, without any agreement, compromise, or concession on our part, either as respects the rights of the public or the individual rights of Mr. Young, Mr. Valiant or Mr. Thomson. Especially we can do nothing, and cannot concur in any action that would concede, for a moment, that Messrs. Young and Valiant are not rightfully in office, or that they have done any unlawful act, or that Mr. Thomson, in acting in obedience to their order, was acting otherwise than in the proper discharge of the duties of his office as sheriff of Baltimore city.

2. At the same time we freely admit, as we have always admitted, that upon the refusal of the Mayor of the city, and of Messrs. Hindes and Wood to deliver over to the possession and control of Messrs. Young and Valiant, as police commissioners, the only peaceful remedy will be an application to the Superior Court of Baltimore city for a mandamus, based on their legal title, with which we insist they were clothed *de jure*, by their appointments, commission and qualification according to law ; and we further insist, that when they opened an office as police commissioners, and performed the official act of commanding the sheriff to summon the *posse comitatus*, and demanded from Messrs. Hindes and Wood the

possession of the station-houses and other property appertaining to the city police, they were in the exercise *de facto*, of the lawful powers of their office as police commissioners of Baltimore city.

We deprecate the possibility of any outbreak in any way that would or might produce a disturbance in our city, and we shall advise the pursuit of the remedy by mandamus, instead of force, as a mode of obtaining possession of the property appertaining to the police board ; but we cannot advise any such action as will acknowledge the right of Messrs. Hindes and Wood to act in any manner as the members of the board of police of Baltimore city.

The case was then proceeded with, and Mr. Alexander said the great question in the case was the question of jurisdiction. In the case of a person committed to jail by a court of exclusive criminal jurisdiction, can any other judge revise a judgment of that court? Assuming that you can hear the case, the next question is: Do the papers on their face state a *prima facie* case sufficient to be accepted by the court and made the basis of its action ? The truth of the return may be inquired into, but the truth of the facts are not for the consideration of the judge—otherwise your Honor might assume to yourself the entire criminal jurisdiction of the city, acting both as judge and jury.

Judge Bartol said he could not determine questions before they arose. It would be quite irregular in him to explain to counsel the course they should pursue. If the pleadings are made up he was ready to proceed with the case.

Considerable time was spent by counsel in preparing additional pleadings ; after which they agreed that no further pleadings should be introduced, but the evidence should be taken subject to exceptions, &c.

Judge Bartol said, the question to be determined is, ought the prisoners now to be enlarged—and whether there. is now probable cause for the arrest of those persons ? The parties supporting the return must show it.

With the assent of counsel and Judge Bartol, Messrs. Thomson, Young and Valiant were allowed their parole.

THE EVIDENCE FOR RESPONDENTS.

The respondents first offered the warrants of arrest as proof of probable cause. They then called—

Wm. C. Crone, sworn.—Is Deputy Sheriff ; served the warrants of arrest against Messrs. Valiant and Young about 11 o'clock on Saturday, November 3d ; went immediately to the headquarters of the new Commissioners, on North street ; there was a great crowd there ; got a hack and brought Messrs. Young and Valiant to the Court house ; the crowd on North street was just the same as is in front of the newspaper offices when the people are waiting for news. The Sheriff had sworn in about sixty men when he was arrested; they were ordered to keep quiet, and told that they were to protect the headquarters of the new Commissioners; they went up in squads of four or five at a time. Marshall Carmichael said he had orders to clear the Court house; there was a crowd of one hundred or more on the stairway and passages. The old police ordered everybody out of the Court house; there was no confusion until the old police ordered them out; witness had an order from the new Commissioners to sign from Sheriff Thomson, to summon 2,000 men as *posse comitatus* to protect their rooms; the Commissioners afterwards said 100 were enough; the Sheriff selected the men from those whom witness summoned; Mr. Amos and himself summoned them; did not know any political test in selecting them; a good many of them he judged would like to become police officers.

Cross-examined—The Police Commissioners were preparing to attend to business in their office; there was no violent or riotous conduct among the men in the Sheriff's office; there was no riotous demonstration at the office of the Police Commissioners; saw nobody struck.

William Fuller sworn—Had a note from Mr. Maund to come up to the Criminal Court; was sworn before the Judge. This witness then repeated the testimony given by him in the Criminal Court on Saturday last. Mr. Valiant said he was going to ask in a civil way of Messrs. Hindes and Wood to deliver up, then, if they did not he would take it by a *posse comitatus;* witness told him he had better consult Mrs. Valiant, Mr. Valiant said he had already consulted Mrs. Valiant and she had advised not to take the office.

Cross-examined.—Received a note from Mr. Maund, earnestly requesting him to call on him; did not report the conversation with Valiant to Mr. Maund or the Police Commissioners; received afterwards a second note; witness was not a volunteer in the case; never spoke of Mr. Young as having said anything to him on the subject; Mr. Valiant used the word "we" in conversing with witness.

By Judge Bartol.—Mr. Valiant said to him, we would go down to the old commissioners' office, and, if necessary, have a *posse comitatus* and put them out; I mentioned the word mandamus. Mr. V. said; "We want no mandamus; if the *posse* cannot put them out, then we have the Government forces."

Thomas Sewell Ball sworn.—Was present when the conversation took place between Mr. Valiant and Mr. Fuller, on Friday afternoon. (This witness then repeated the conversation as testified to by Mr. Fuller.) Mr. Valiant said he was sorry he was appointed, but as long as he was appointed, he was going to have the office; witness gave the same testimony before Judge Bond.

George W. Taplor sworn.—Is secretary to the Police Board, No. 12, Holliday street; witness testified to the different visits of Messrs. Young and Valiant to the commissioners' room; the Board of Police has a seal; the record of proceedings was in possession of the old Board; Messrs. Young and Valiant visited the office twice on Saturday; there was an immense crowd about the office; they handed witness a note for Messrs. Hindes and Wood.

Heie Mr. Stirling read the note, wich was a demand for the office, books, papers, &c.

Cross-examined—When they called on Friday, Mr. Hindes was present; thinks the Mayor and Mr. Hindes had an interview; witness met Young and Valiant, by direction of the full Board; told them that they could not see the Board personally; told them if they made a communication in writing it would be promptly answered—no answer has been received up to this time; witness wrote the note to Mr. Fuller at the request of one of our counsel; the arrest of Messrs. Valiant and Young was not made at the suggestion of Messrs. Hindes and Wood; Mr. Clayton told witness the remarks of Mr. Valiant to Mr. Fuller; the matter of the letter was communicated to the counsel of the Board, who told him to write the note to Mr. Fuller; is at present acting às Secretary of the Board; the Board; is now drawing money when they want it; there is a special fund, arising from fines, in the hands of the Commissioners; they are using it now, as it is wanted.

George C. Maund sworn—Is State's Attorney of Baltimore city. It was at his suggestion, based on the information he received, that Judge Bond sent for the Sheriff; asked him if he was swearing in men, and for what purpose. The Sheriff said that it was to keep the peace. Judge Bond told him he must desist, or he would have him arrested as a rioter. Shortly afterwards there was considerable noise in the hall of the court house; Judge Bond asked witness to see what occasioned it; witness went out and saw a large number of mem coming down the steps from the Sheriff's office, wearing a white ribbon, and others going up without the ribbon; went into the Sheriff's office through the crowd of men; told Mr. Thomson that he was requested by Judge Bond to ask him if he was swearing in men; Mr. Thomson said he was swearing them in solely to keep the peace, and that it was under the written directions of the commissioners appointed by Governor Swann; witness reported the facts to Judge Bond, and upon that and his application the court issued a warrant for the arrest of the Sheriff. There was a great deal of confusion in the hall of the court house; he felt apprehensive that there would be a breach of the peace; he asked the court, after Messrs. Fuller and Ball had testified in the matter, to issue

8

the warrants in his official capacity; he asked the Court to issue warrants for Messrs. Young and Valiant; the court ordered them to give bail to keep the peace; there was no effort made by them to examine witnesses in their behalf; the parties declined to give the bail.

Cross-examined.—Witness made no affidavit in the case; the Judge was on the bench; saw no actual evidence; in his judgment, the act of swearing in men by the Sheriff was an unlawful assemblage. Mr. Maund then related the circumstances under which the warrants for the arrest of Messrs. Young and Valiant were issued.

Robert E. Eccleston sworn.—Is a policeman; was at the Western station on Saturday morning; saw two men on the street with white ribbons; one was named James Rhodes, and both were intoxicated; spoke to James Rhodes, he was formerly on our force; did'nt know the other; witness was not at the court house that day; thinks he saw these men about the middle of the day.

Mr. Stirling presented a copy of the Baltimore American, of Monday, 5th of November, containing an order from the new board of police commissioners to the marshals and police force, to refrain from obeying any other board, &c., and asked to have the same admitted as testimony.

Thos. H. Carmichael sworn.—Is marshal of the police force of Baltimore; was in the court house on Saturday, 3d November, in the exercise of his duty, with forty officers, and cleared the court house out, and selected some good officers, placed them at the doors with orders to let no one in unless on business; the court house was packed with people; it was impossible to pass through the crowd without pushing; didn't remain long in the court house; great crowds were on Baltimore street at that time, the largest crowd witness ever saw in the square was on that day; has seen larger crowds at mass meetings there; the crowd on Baltimore street extended from Frederick to Light street; Holliday street was also greatly crowded; had a large police force on these streets, every available man being sent there; the crowd was pushing around, and appeared considerably excited; on North street the crowd was very great, extending from Baltimore to Fayette street; sent no officers into the Criminal Court; saw no one knocked down in the rotunda of the court house; saw no one draw a pistol there.

A discussion arose between counsel as to the admissibility of evidence; by the witness in relation to his knowledge of certain arms in South Charles street, and his action in reference thereto, on Monday, the 5th November, 1866.

The court ruled the testimony inadmissible.

Examination resumed.—Witness saw persons loading muskets on the 5th instant.

Cross-examination.—Does not know the hour that witness

brought his force to the court house; did not know Messrs. Valiant and Young were arrested at the time; Mr. Hindes told witness to take a force to the court house; over a hundred policemen had been stationed on Baltimore street; the regular force is about 358, in addition to which there were 700 special officers summoned by order of Messrs. Hindes and Wood; can't tell whether the specials had been summoned before Gov. Swann had removed the old board; they were summoned before Saturday. Some were summoned on Friday and some on the Thursday preceding; on Thursday wit; ness thinks the first written order was given for special officers; the magistrates of the stations swore in the specials-Justice Whalen, Showacre, Spicer, Hebden and Johnson swore them in; can't tell how long it would take to summon 700 men; the board gives the order to the marshal and he to the captains, and thence through the officers those summoned are brought in; the crowd in the Criminal Court room on Saturday was not as large as the crowd present now.

Mr. Stirling read from the Baltimore American of the 2d, a communication from Messrs. Young and Valiant, relating to their plan of action in regard to the men of the force, &c., which was offered as testimony.

Archibald Stirling sworn.—Witness was in the Criminal Court on Saturday, at the time of the issue of the warrants for the new commissioners and sheriff; at 4 o'clock there was an immense crowd in front of the court house; went to the window and saw three or four hundred men rushing in an excited manner up Lexington street towards Charles street; the court room became emptied in consequence of the excitement and desire to see what was the matter; a short time before witness had left the office of the Commissioners on Holliday street, in front of which an immense crowd had also gathered; saw a large crowd in the Court House alley, among them two squads marching shoulder to shoulder up the alley into the court house; they were rough looking men; went back to the Criminal Court room and heard a great uproar outside, a noise of rushing to and fro; the impression made on witness was that there was going to be a seizure of the court house; saw a bailiff arrest a man, who struggled violently; it was thought by several gentlemen in the court room that an attack was going to be made on the Criminal Court; Judge Bond told witness that he had sent for a police force to protect the court house; the noise was so great that the court could transact no business; this occurred about half an hour before the warrants were issued, in the neighborhood of 12 or 1 o'clock; to witness it appeared that the crowd on Holliday street were, of one stripe, and the one around the court house of another; everything looked like a collision between these two crowds; witness was not sworn on Saturday before Judge Bond.

The testimony for the respondents was announced as closed. The following testimony was elicited on behalf of the petitioners:

TESTIMONY FOR PETITIONERS.

John M. Carter sworn.—Is Secretary of State of the Commonwealth of Maryland ; has a copy of the order dismissing the old board of police. [The order was then read by Mr. Carter, being listened to by the large crowd with the closest attention.] Excepted to by respondents. After the passing of the order, witness notified the commissioners, serving each with a copy, together with a letter to them. [Which was read.]

On the evening of November 1, about 6½ o'clock, witness went to the office of Messrs. Hindes and Wood, on Holliday street, and in the presence of Thomas S. Alexander, J. J. Alexander, Archibald Stirling, W. H. Taylor and Mayor Chapman, served the original on the board.

[The commissions of Messrs. Valiant and Young were produced and read.] These commissions were brought to Baltimore by witness about noon on Friday, 2d inst. Mr. Leary, private Secretary to the Governor, notified these gentlemen, and they went to the Governor's residence, where they received their commissions.

The qualifications of the commissioners in the test book of the Superior Court were offered in evidence.

Cross-examined.—The words "decision of character" were inserted in the commissions by witness without consultation with any one; it is not the usual formulary; has never used them before; witness left Baltimore on the 7 A. M. train on Friday, 2d inst., and returned by special train to Annapolis Junction, and thence by regular train, reaching Baltimore about 12.45 P. M.; Messrs. Young and Valiant had received no intimation of their appointments until they were informed on Friday; the commissions were signed and sealed at Annapolis on Friday morning, the 2d inst.; these are the only commissions filled up; others in blank, signed and sealed previously, were brought to the city for emergencies, they are now at the Governor's house, in this city; Governor Swann came to the city on the same train with witness; there may have been names in the heading of these commissions in blank, but the bodies were not filled up; the reason of this was, that everything might be ready in the event of any emergency arising from declination of the appointees.

The witness explained at some length the ordinary manner in which commissions usually reach the appointees, &c.

Re-examined.—After the commissions were delivered to Messrs. Young and Valiant they started to qualify; witness accompanied them; we went to Mr. Latrobe's office, where a form of oath was made out; thence to the Superior Court room, where the Commissioners qualified; then we went to the office of the Board of Police Commissioners, on Holliday street; at the gate they were met by Deputy Marshal Manly; being unable to get in, they went to the Mayor's office, but failed to get in there; this occurred between 3 and 4 o'clock, on Friday; there was quite a crowd on the pavement—among them several policemen, and a number of the latter were in the front yard attached to the Commissioners' building.

Benjamin Swearer sworn.—Witness was at the Sheriff's office on Saturday when the arrest took place; the police came rushing up stairs with clubs and billies, saying "Get out of here, you s—s of b—s;" witness thought he was going to get "some;" all had been quiet until the police came; witness had been a police officer, but resigned on Monday, when he was told he had better do so by Captain Lynch.

Cross-examined.—Witness had not been on duty for several weeks, having been sick; witness had been at the new Commissioners' before he went to the Sheriff's; went with some ten others to the Sheriff's to have them sworn in; about 11 A. M. went to the new Commissioners' office; had been, earlier in the day, at Mr. Schley's office, where the Commissioners were in consultation, where he helped to keep the crowd out; about half-past 9 o'clock first went to see the new Commissioners, and had some conversation with them.

John Thompson sworn.—Witness swore the most of the posse in on Saturday las ; is a Deputy Sheriff; was present when the police burst into the office in a most riotous manner, with deadly weapons; everything had previously been perfectly quiet. [The oath administered by the Sheriff to those sworn in, was produced and read.]

Cross-examined.—Is a brother of the Sheriff, and has been a Deputy since his brother has been in office; witness was a candidate for the Legislature at the late election, and is under the impression that he was elected; witness passed upon the characters of those sworn in as the posse, and would have rejected any one whom he considered unfit, does not recollect whether he swore in John Reese; the time occupied in the swearing was about three-quarters of an hour, some fifty or sixty having been sworn; the approach to the Sheriff's office was blocked up by men waiting to be sworn, but there was'nt the slightest disturbance until the police came with billies uplifted.

The petitioners announced their testimony as closed.

MORE TESTIMONY FOR RESPONDENTS.

The respondent then offered the following additional testimony :

Sergeant Hand sworn.—Was one of the police force which went to the court house on Saturday last; first went with three men, and was insulted by some men at the entrance with white ribbons, who said: "There go the played out sons of bitches;" then went for forty men, who were ordered to clear the court house; the steps leading to the Sheriff's office were filled with a very disorderly crowd, and witness had to climb up by the banisters; the police were orderly; did not see any billies, or hear them use any foul language; saw Swearer there; did not see him doing anything; saw several men with white ribbons around the court house; all the police tried to get up the stairs; Marshal Carmichael ordered them to clear the court house.

Cross-examined.—The disorder consisted in making a noise; the men did not strike at the police; did not see any one thrown down stairs by the police; there might have been some thrown down and witness might not have seen them; witness did not go into the Sheriff's office.

Officer James H. Lamden sworn.—Was stationed at the Police Commissioners' office on Saturday, at the fence; the new Commissioners came down there twice, and the second time Swearer and three men with white ribbons, at the head of a crowd, came around through Orange street, and took a stand on the pavement, in front of the building; they were hurrahing for Johnson and Swann, and very noisy: Swearer kept the gangway clear from the hack of the new Commissioners to the gate as well as he could.

Cross-examined.—About thirty men were stationed at the fence, and others were back in the yard; witness had been there for some time before the Commissioners came. There were special police there at the second visit of the Police Commissioners.

Officer Ramsey sworn.—Was one of the squad which went to the court house under orders to clear it; the place was crowded, and a good deal of difficulty was had in getting them out; saw no billies used; did not go into the Sheriff's office.

The counsel then deciding to argue the case, a discussion arose as to which side was entitled to open and close the argument, the court deciding that the right rested with petitioners.

The court then adjourned until next morning at ten o'clock, and the Commissioners and Sheriff, being in the custody of the court, were permitted to go to their homes until morning, when it was required for them to be present at the court room.

ARGUMENT OF MR. LATROBE.

John H. B. Latrobe, Esq., opened the argument on behalf of the petitioners. He stated that he would be followed by

Mr. Stockbridge, for the respondents; Mr. Horwitz would
next argue the case of Sheriff Thomson, and incidentally the
cases of the commissioners; Messrs. Rogers and Alexander
would then further ague the case of the respondents, and Mr.
Schley would conclude for the petitioners.

"The decision of Governor Swann," said Mr. Latrobe,
"gave to the commissioners of his appointment the instant
and immediate possession of the franchise, the property and
muniments of the office being reserved, perhaps, for after consideration. Messrs. Young and Valiant were committed on
two charges. They were held to bail upon these charges in
twenty-five thousand dollars. Upon these commitments, our
clients being sent to prison, they petition for a writ of habeas
corpus. Your Honor decided yesterday that it was for the
other side to maintain the return by showing probable cause
for the imprisonment of our clients. Testimony was endeavored to be produced to support that return. We were
then on the eve of a most exciting and important election.
We were under the domination of some 5,000 men. Under
their rule, but opposed to them in political sentiment, were
some 35,000 persons. They are a high-spirited people, enter-
prising in their patriotism from the time they defended their
city against a foreign foe. They were great in all the arts
and sciences, and elevated in all their ideas of social and
business life. It would not have been wonderful under the
circumstances of the appointment by Governor Swann of
Messrs. Young and Valiant to the office of police commissioners, that they should have resisted the unjust rule of so
small a minority.

It would not have been surprising if the people had taken
the new commissioners upon their shoulders, and carried them
triumphantly into the office of the old ones. But honorable
to the people of Baltimore, they abstained from violence, and
it will form a bright page in the history of Baltimore that
they were entirely obedient to law and order. There was
never exhibited similar obedience to the law. Every order
given by the new commissioners was accompanied with in-
structions to obey the law. That is sufficient to show that
there was no probable cause of riot. We have the evidence
of our brethren of the bar on the other side, and that of police
officers, although perhaps slightly biased in their opinions,
and there is nothing in their testimony to show probability
of riot. The most they have testified to is that there was a
crowd collected near the court-house to see what was going on.
But the same result would be produced any day by a drum
and fife. There were no blows struck—no pistols fired. The
most that was testified to was that some of the posse comitatus said to some of the old police, "You are all played out."
The police were the men who created the disturbance. There
were men sufficient to have overcome them with a single

tramp, if they had been disposed. There is no doubt that the crowd could have thrown out the forty policemen from the court house windows. But they were obedient to authority, and respected the law. It was not the forty men with batons—it was the law, that restrained them.

It is only necessary to refer to these facts to show how idle was the assertion that a riot was impending. What was the conspiracy? James Young and Wm. T. Valiant conspiring to carry out the duties they were appointed to perform? No. The real conspirators were the old commissioners, who conspired to resist the law under the legal advice of some of our legal friends on the other side, who should have advised them better. My friend next me (Mr. Alexander,) at that particular time, found himself unhappily and unwittingly ignorant of law.

[Here there were demonstrations of applause, which were rebuked by Judge Bartol, and which did not again occur during the day,

Mr. Latrobe said he referred to the testimony and the circumstances of the case to show how utterly futile is the argument of probable cause. Suppose there was probable cause, out of what did it arise? That brings us to the root of the matter. If that probable cause arose from the acts of those who were carrying out their authority, they were not responsible. If they were authorized to act as commissioners, they were authorized to appoint officers under them. If there was a rush to obtain the places of policemen under the new commissioners, or to see the new commissioners, it amounted not to rioting; or if riot resulted from the resistance made by the old commissioners to the authority of the new ones, then the former are responsible.

We are, therefore, thrown at once upon the validity of the appointment of Messrs. Young and Valiant, and of their authority to act by virtue of their aqpointment. (Mr. Latrobe then reviewed the law establishing the police force of the city.] The power possessed by the police, board is unpredented. It was irresponsible except to the General Assembly. It had the broadest and amplest powers. That was in 1860. In 1861 sad occurrences took place in Baltimore, in connection with the beginning of the unhappy troubles of our country. The Governor of the State found the whole police authority of Baltimore vested in a board. He was powerless to control them. The city was placed under martial law. The Legislature, meeting in 1862, determined that the Governor of the State should not be in subjection to the board of police. Some of our friends on the other side were members of the committee that was [appointed to alter the law, and gave the Governor the power to remove the commissioners for official misconduct. Our friends will argue, perhaps, that the courts should be resorted to for the purpose.

of inducting the new commissioners before the old commissioners were removed. Was this the legislative intent? It was necessary to act promptly in certain exigencies. Could tedious legal proceedings have been intended under such circumstances? The very object of the law would have been defeated. It never could have been the intention of the Legislature to compel the Governor to resort to the courts. An apt illustration was the refusal to produce the police commissioners until after three days. There the mischief was continued through the day of the election, thus defeating the very intention of the law. If it had been necessary for the Governor to resort to the courts in 1861, the consequences would have been far more distressing. Still, through the intervention of Providence at the last election, the right has been maintained.

It never could have been the legislative intent to refer the Governor to the courts. Our friends cannot produce a case where the Governor is authorized to act in a specific manner, and his action has been disregarded. In the Code the Governor is required to perform certain duties. In the event of any complaint being made against any civil or military officer whom the Governor can remove, he shall summon witnesses to inquire into the facts, and all means are provided for a full and impartial hearing. The law existed previously that defined his duties and mode of action. Having the complaint before him in this case, he investigated the whole case. But that was out of abundant caution. I hold that he was authorized upon view, upon an affidavit, to have removed these commissioners and appointed new ones, and he was responsible only to the Legislature. But in the mode of investigation he exercised his authority lawfully. When this appointment was made, and the commissioners qualified under this appointment, they were *ipso facto* the board of police. Not that they had possession of the property, but they had the right, the full right, to such office and property. On the 2nd of November, Messrs. Young and Valiant became police commissioners of Baltimore. The order removing the old commissioners was passed on Thursday, and they were notified of the fact. The new board denied admission to them on the following day. On Saturday they called again, and they were arrested. Hence these proceedings. The removal, with notice of it, vacated the office. The appointment, with the qualification, installed the new board. It was the duty of the old commissioners to have known the correct law and complied with it. On the appearance of the new commissioners the old board should have received them on Friday afternoon, and availed themselves only of time to close up their affairs. That was their duty, no matter what were the interest involved. That was their duty, if the law is as I have stated it, and I claim that such is the law. The reports

9

of the papers telegraphed to Baltimore on Thursday before
noon the fact that the removal would be made. The old
board and all Baltimore knew it on Thursday. But the next
day they received official notice of the fact. Yet on Thursday they were summoning 700 special policemen while the
new board only called for 100 men. They continued this on
Friday. They were preparing an army to resist the law.
Let them explain that. Mark the contrast between their
actions and the actions of the new commissioners. Who are
the rioters? Who should have been committed to prison?
The application to Judge Bond for warrants should have been
made for the arrest of Messrs. Hindes and Wood, and his
Honor the Mayor. Instead of preparing such a resistance,
it was their duty to let in the new commissioners, and bow
to the law. It is said they did not do so because they feared
a riot. Their object was to hold over the election, with the
belief that they would be successful in that election, and thus
hold us for four years longer in subjection. The whole question turns upon the validity of the appointment, and the
rights secured by such appointment. In accordance with the
past decisions, you have the right to go behind the commitment. We ask you to look at the circumstances of the time
and to the testimony in that connection. These men have
been imprisoned and are still under constructive restraint.
We want no compromise. We want them liberated, because
they have the right to be liberated.

Mr. Latrobe concluded his argument by quoting from the
16th chapter of the Acts of the Apostles, verse 35 to 40
inclusive, as applicable to the case.

REMARKS OF MR. STOCKBRIGE.

The prisoners are detained under a lawful commitment of
a court exercising jurisdiction in such matters. The case was
laid open and the whole subject is now before you. It is
against all law and precedent that so great a latitude shall be
allowed in the trial upon a writ of habeas corpus as has been
claimed and availed of in the argument of my friend on the
other side. The Code gives to the courts of this State and
city and the judges out of court jurisdiction over the whole
State in matters of habeas corpus. Though a judge of the
highest court of the State, your power is the same as in every
other court, and with all the other judges of the State. You
have no appellate or reviewing power. You cannot revise
or reverse the return other than to examine if it is legally
issued. The effect of it would be to enable your Honor to
reverse or revise the judgment of all the courts of criminal
jurisdiction in the State. and the court with jurisdiction over
him would be baffled in all his efforts to bring an offender to
justice. Mr. Stockbridge quoted a number of legal authorities in support of his view.

In Green's Reports, second volume, page 312, it is recorded that if a judge at chambers can inquire into and decide the right of a plaintiff to arrest the defendant, there shall he terminate his inquiries. Not a single case sustains the contrary doctrine. The writ is a legal and proper one. The court has competent jurisdiction. I refer to fourth McCord; reports to 1 Watts, 66; to 2 Casey, 9; to Hurd on Habeas Corpus, p. 332, 335.

Unless aided by the Assembly of Maryland in this case, you are limited to the inquiry. Was there a proper legal mittimus under which these parties are held? The Code provides that the party may controvert the truth of the return, or plead to the matters alleged therein. The act of 1813, chapter 135, contains the law up to that time. Under that act, the recognized law of Maryland, until the adoption of the Code, the verity of the return alone could be impeached. The truth of the return may be controverted, or plead matters repugnant, or avoid it by showing that there was not sufficient legal cause for the detention. The return alone is drawn in question. In the act of 1809, it is said the truth of the return may be controverted. Chancellor Kelly understood the law as I have read it. The law goes no further than to say the return may be controverted.

The Code was designed to simply embody the scattered enactments of the State. It does not give appellate power to every judge of Maryland over every other judge. The case 13, Md., 636, does not conflict with the statement of the law. Where the law is clear, the argument from inconvenience cannot avail. A defendant cannot be discharged from the commitment by reason of any error in the original proceedings. A writ of habeas corpus is not a writ of error. At common law the return imputed absolute verity. It could not be traversed or its truth inquired out. The act of 1813 authorizes all these things. If a party is convicted by legal process, he is denied the benefit of the writ. If the judgment is by a competent court, that judgment cannot be inquired into because of error. The law is not affected by the statute of Maryland, or by any decision in this State. The jurisdiction of the Criminal Court is not fixed by the acts of Assembly.— The twenty-ninth article of the Code determines its jurisdiction. It has jurisdiction of all crimes and felonies in Baltimore. It has exclusive jurisdiction, and its decision concludes the whole until they are reversed upon a writ of error. The judge of the court is at all times a conservator of the peace. It has the power to commit to jail in default of bail, and to require bail when a prima facia is made out. There can be no controversy with reference to the power of that court in this matter.

The return in this case sets forth two different commitments, one to answer for a crime, the other in default of bail to keep the peace; one is a commitment on mesne process, the other upon final judgment. All proceedings entering between the beginning and ending of a case, are mesne process. The rights of these parties do not make a question in this case. I shall not discuss the power or action of the Governor of the State in the matter of the trial of the Police Commissioners. It does not come in question here. The record is not before us.

A single order was produced, which was the ultimate order, in the view of the opposite side, but that does not come before us here for confirmation or appeal in this proceeding.— That question must come up in an entirely different proceeding. As to the Legislature, it was their design no take the police force from all political influences. It was never designed that it should be placed at the disposal of any one man.

In 1862 the old act was repealed and the new one enacted, and Messrs Wood and Hindes were appointed under that act. Mr. Wood was re-elected in 1864 by a different body of men. Still later Mr. Hindes was re-elected by another Legislature, thus deciding their fitness and uprightness to hold their office. Before the proceedings at Annapolis these commissioners were *de jure* and *de facto* the Board of Police of Baltimore. One man again assumes to control this force for purposes I will not mention. The irregularity of these proceedings will be discussed at another time.

But whatever may have been the justice of the claims of the opposite side, no claim to an office gives the claimant a right to seize possession of the office by the strong arm of physical force. The first act of the new Commissioners was to issue a proclamation without consulting another member of the Board, and without giving to the community their authority by such or in any other manner.

By reason of this and other acts, one of the new commissioners threatening to take a posse and appeal to force, there was ample cause for arresting them. An appeal to force is necessarily riot and bloodshed. They attempted to carry out this programme, instead of calling their own police to their assistance.

REMARKS OF MR. HORWITZ.

Although I appear more particularly on behalf of the Sheriff of Baltimore city, but yet. inasmuch as whatever was done by him was done by virtue of an order received from the commissioners appointed by the Governor, it will be necessary for the purposes of my argument, not to confine myself to the action of the Sheriff, but to discuss the authority under which he acted, and the right of the commissioners to act under their authority.

In the case of such palpable outrage as has been perpetra-

ted upon the Sheriff, it is difficult to speak with calmness.—
But I shall endeavor to discuss the subject uninfluenced by
feeling. The able and eloquent argument submitted by my
friend Mr. Latrobe covered entirely the case of the commissioners, and presented clearly the relative position of the ac-
tors in this miserable drama. In the Sheriff's case there were
facts presented by the evidence which require, on the part of
your Honor, the severest reprobation of those who were connected therewith. You may search the annals of jurispru-
dence from the earliest records down to the present day, without omitting the period of Charles the Second, and you will
find no similar case on record.

But before I proceed to present the facts in this case, allow
me to inquire if it is true that if a party is incarcerated in
our jail, and the commitment is regular upon its face, and by
the authority of a competent officer, that he must lie there?
It cannot be, and it is not so, in this State, by your own authority, and that of the Court of Appeals, who approved of
your decision in the case of Maulsby. There are numerous
cases in the books sustaining that, [Here the counsel referred to several authorities.] This is not the case of the execution of a judgment, but in regard to a commitment, which is
mesne process, there can be no doubt upon the question of
the right to go behind a commitment. On page 637 of 13th
Maryland, you yourself have said "that it is competent for
the judge, notwithstanding the warrant of commitment is in
due form and by a competent officer, to determine upon the
proof exhibited the real ground of the accusation."

The cases referred to by the counsel on the other side are
cases of judgment on contempt, and of execution issued upon
judgments rendered. But in reply to all the cases cited on
this point, I stand upon your own decision in the case of
Maulsby. To say that we cannot inquire into the cause of
commitment, and ascertain if there be sufficient ground therefor, is to destroy the privilege of the great writ of habeas corpus, of which we boast so much. But if we were compelled
to rely upon the commitment and on the papers returned in
this case, the defects in the case of the Sheriff are palpable
and numerous. In violation of the Constitution of the United
States and of our own bill of rights, the bench warrant for the
arrest of the Sheriff was issued without any oath to support
it, and he was dragged from his office to the Criminal Court.
Had the Judge of that Court any right to issue that writ? By
the 26th Article of the Declaration of Rights it is declared
that all warrants without oath or affirmation, "to seize the
property or arrest the person of any citizen, are grievous and
oppressive." And yet this high officer is dragged from his
office and from the quiet exercise of the duties of his position
without the sanction of an oath, (3d Bailly, 38.)

While in the very execution of the process, through his

deputies, of arresting Messrs. Valiant and Young, the Sheriff himself was arrested because the Judge heard a noise overhead and the State's Attorney got a little excited and nervous (1st Tyler, 444.)

When the sheriff reached the court room he was astounded to find that he had been arrested on a charge of riot. A more peaceable assemblage of persons summoned by the sheriff in obedience to law, and bound to attend, could not have been found. According to the evidence there was not the slightest tumult in the sheriff's office nor in its surroundings, until the police force came there, and then no resistance was made to them. Some few remonstrated, and said to the police officers, "do not interfere with us, we have just been sworn in as conservators of the peace." But the police, with their batons and billies soon disposed of the unarmed and unresisting *posse.*

The judge then required of the sheriff bail in the sum of $5,000 to answer the charge of riot, without a particle of evidence before him to justify the outrage. Having this officer before them, and without any evidence or any oath, the judge then passes the most extraordinary order on record. This petty magistrate of a police force attempts to settle the question of the appointment, of the police commissioners, and who are entitled to hold office. This magistrate, not competent according to the Constitution of the State, to determine the law in a case of the larceny of five dollars, for, according to the Constitution, the jury is made sole judge of the law of criminal cases—erects himself into a court of equity, with power to issue an injunction or to grant a mandamus.

We have heard a great deal of talk about riot and danger, and the peace of this great city, but as yet we have seen no one, except Mr. Maund and Mr. Stirling, who appears to have had the slightest fear of a riot in the city. Their efforts to get up the idea of danger and tumult and fear, have utterly failed; they have not been sustained by the proof before your Honor. Why, then, was this order passed?

The sheriff had received an order from the commissioners newly appointed to summon a *posse comitatus* for the preservation of the peace and quiet of the city, and for no other purpose. Every man summoned was sworn to preserve the peace, and aid in maintaining the quiet of the city.

Was the Sheriff right in obeying the order directed to him? This, of course, depends on the authority of the commissioners. Were they authorized to issue the order?

The commissioners appeared before the Sheriff with their commission, sealed with the great seal of the State, and he was made acquainted with the fact that they had qualified under it. The great seal of a State proves itself, and by the law of nations is to be recognized the world over. And is the document not to have force with one of the officers of the very State whose seal it bears? [Wendell, 484, 7 Shipley, 650.] Coming thus supported, they direct to him the order that has been read in evidence. Under a penalty of $5000 he is bound to obey the order of the Commissioners, and, therefore, had to decide for himself upon the validity of that order. And he was right in the conclusion to which he came. They are the Commissions *de jure*, by virtue of their appointment. It is useless to discuss the right of the Governor to remove for official misconduct, and to appoint others in their place. For the sake of this argument it is conceded by the counsel who just addressed the Court. And they were also the Commissioners *de facto*. It is not like the case of the Librarian, who cannot act without the Library. They may establish their offices and station-houses and telegraphs where they please. They may adopt a seal. They may act without the aid of the old Commissioners. They were then Commissioners *de jure et de facto*. They had opened their office; they had issued this very order.

In this state of the case, what is done? They have the Sheriff before them, and then, without any complaint or cause of complaint, they pass an order requiring the Sheriff to give bond not to obey the law. The law says he shall obey the order of the Commissioners of Police under a penalty of $5000 for disobedience, but the Criminal Court says you must give a bond in a penalty of $20,000 to disobey the law and to pay the fine of $5000. And this order the justice of a police court passes of his own motion, without any complaint, and decides in effect, that the appointment of the Governor is invalid, and that the Commissioners had no power to control the Sheriff. In this predicament the Sheriff had no alternative but to go to jail, and there he has been ever since.

What more do they do! They not only arrest him without oath, in violation of the Constitution and Bill of Rights, but they take him to jail on a commitment that does not charge the offence, and afterwards, when the petition for habeas corpus had been filed, and the writ served, they issue and lodge with the warden a new commitment, charging the supposed offence.

The matter was so monstrous that it bordered on the ridiculous, and was talked of on the public thoroughfares as a good political joke, and parties were congratulated on having made a first rate euchre.

I am not very familiar with this game, but I am told by those who understand it that the party that holds two knaves and an ass, or an ace, as I believe they call it, is sure to gain his point. I am certain that the party on the other side held no such hand, for they lost the game. They may have supposed that by holding the two commissioners and the Sheriff, their hand was invincible; but I think before we are

done with them that they will find that they have played at
the wrong game throughout.

When we express our indignation in terms scarcely ade-
quate to the outrage, what answer do they make to us ? The
answer they give this day is, that we are shut out from looking at the truth—that we cannot go behind the papers that
they have brought into court, but must remain in jail until
discharged by the grand jury. It is useless to cite authority
on a question like that. Common sense tells us that it would
be a libel on the age and country in which we live to allow
such principle to prevail.

At the conclusion of Mr. Horwitz's argument, the court
took a recess for one hour and a half. Upon the reassem-
bling of the court, at 3 o'clock, Mr. Schley gave the usual
notice to counsel on the other side of several legal authorities
he proposed to use in concluding the argument of the case.

ARGUMENT OF MR. ROGERS.

Alexander Rogers, Esq., the deputy State's attorney for
Baltimore city, said he felt a grave responsibility in appearing
to represent the State, and but that able counsel were asso-
ciated with him, he should regard it as a fearful responsibility for him to assume. He thought that it was only necessary to show the court that the commitments had been made
out properly and emanated from a proper court ; that the
question would be examined as to the jurisdiction of the judge
sitting in habeas corpus. The old law said that if there were
errors in the returns, the remedy was by an action for per-
jury. The rule was afterwards changed, so that when the
return was traversed, an examination *ex parte* could be gone
into. He maintained that the court could not review a writ
of habeas corpus, unless the court had criminal jurisdiction.
He denied the power of a judge to go behind a warrant of
commitment, and quoted and commented upon a long list of
authorities to show that the precedents in Maryland were in
conflict with the fixed and established rules of law. The action of a judge cannot be reviewed on a writ of habeas corpus
—the discretion of a judge in the case cannot be reviewable.
Mr. Rogers expressed his regret at entering upon an almost
boundless field of discussion, but it was unavoidable. The
counsel on the other side have sufficiently indicated by their
manner and unfavorable opinion of the motives of the district
attorney and himself in the course they had pursued, but he
had no reason to distrust the correctness of the legal opinions
which they had given in the matter. He believed that by
their action they had saved the country from the horrors of a
civil strife, which would have been awful to contemplate.
However much their motives may be impugned, they have the

testimony of their conscience that they have acted in strict conformity with the law. This is our crown of rejoicing, and no man can deprive us of it.

Mr. R. then discussed the right of forcible induction into office and the law of habeas corpus, and illustrated his views by reference to the legal enactments and historical examples for several hundred years. Mr. Roger's argument on all the questions raised in the case was very full and exhaustive of the subject, and lasted three hours.

At five o'clock, P. M., the further hearing was postponed until 10 o'clock, A. M., to-morrow.

SATURDAY MORNING, Nov. 10th.

Upon the opening of the cases this morning, Mr. Rogers asked permission to cite a few authorities on behalf of the State to support the ground taken by him that a court could act "upon view" in case of a riot—that it was not only sufficient for the purpose of a warrant, but for the purpose of a conviction, and that commitment in general terms was sufficient. He also stated that if there was an error in the first commitment of the parties, it was a misprision of the clerk, and correctable by the court—that a court of record may commit without form of warrant.

Mr. Schley said the State could not produce any authority for a State's Attorney, deputy or judge to send in a new commitment in the absence of the accused.

ARGUMENT OF MR. ALEXANDER.

Thomas S. Alexander, Esq., said, if I were about to address the popular sense, I should refer to many of the topics discussed by my friends on the other side with so much energy and eloquence. By making a plain statement of a plain case, I could not doubt of my ability to convince my audience the counsel and the court that instead of receiving the public obloquy, the State's attorney and the judge of the Criminal Court deserve the grateful thanks of the country for their prompt and energetic action in the arrest of the parties.

I am satisfied, and I think it is the general sentiment of the community, that had it not been for that action, the sun would have set upon Saturday last upon a scene of riot and massacre and bloodshed. I cannot, however, forget that I am arguing a legal case before a judge of the Court of Appeals. I propose to limit myself to the discussion of questions of law and fact. You have had a description of the events which led to the adoption of the police law of 1861. The present Executive of Maryland, who now seeks to destroy the efficiency of this board, was the head of the police organization in 1860, and it was because of his manipulations of that force that the change was made in the law. The opposing counsel thinks no antecedent case of similar character is to be found in history. They say justly that the Missouri case does not

10

apply here. The conduct of the Governor finds no justification. There was no court open in Missouri before which the case could have been adjudicated. But the courts here are ever open.

The Ju ige of the Superior Court could have been applied to, and from his determination an appeal lies to the Court of Appeals of this State. Our friends on the other side search back to the times of the Stuarts, and they admit that, even in that most degraded epoch of judicial history, they can find no case which can supply a parallel. The wrongs then proceeded from the tyranny of the Executives of that age, sustained by the corrupt judges of their appointment. They They then strove to suppress the charters and our friends have not heard of the proposition to suppress the charter of Baltimore. They would seek by force, disregarding the courts of law and justice, to execute their purposes, and if the physical force of Maryland were not sufficient, they were to call in the army of the United States. They say rightly, no precedent can be found for such enormities as were attempted to be perpetrated by these parties. The Criminal Court is one of exclusive criminal jurisdiction in the city of Baltimore. I refer to Johnson, 358. The legality of a commitment cannot be inquired into and reviewed. A commitment in execution is considered and also a commitment at any stage. The gentlemen concede that after conviction no habeas corpus can be taken out in vacation to review the sentence. Yet, with regard to all mesne process, a judge in vacation can review them. I refer to 5 Johnson, 289. A person convicted at Oyer and Terminer, the judgment could not be controlled by a judge in vacation. The court which commits has jurisdiction of the case, and that is sufficient. When a court of record rightfully assumes jurisdiction over person or property, all other jurisdiction is excluded. It is equally the rule in civil and criminal cases. The court of superior jurisdiction issues a *capias* in debt. The defendant was committed. He sues out a writ of habeas corpus, and wished to show that the commitment did not give sufficient cause for his imprisonment. That is Greene's case, quoted by Stockbridge. In the South Carolina case, given in McCord's Report, it was determined that the regularity of a commitment upon mesne process could not be investigated. The mesne process of a criminal court having exclusive jurisdiction is still more to be respected than in cases of *meum* and *tuum* between citizen and citizen. After a verdict rendered by the jury below, you have the power to review the facts upon whch the conviction was made. That is the conclusion to which the argument of the other side leads. Upon what principle can the commitment of this court of exclusive criminal jurisdiction be reviewed by your Honor sitting in in vacation. Where a justice commits a party upon charg of having committed an offense, there is no court clothed with appellate jurisdiction over that act, save that which results from the habeas corpus. But this writ was never designed to answer the purposes of a writ of error.

If this court had no power to commit upon the charge of conpiracy, let the case proceed to final judgment, and the case can be reviewed upon writ of error. If the legality of this commitment is before you for reviewal, let us see whether we have shown sufficient cause for their detainer. The law of riots and unlawful assemblies does not apply here. It is conspiracy that constitutes the offense here. It is that offense · by which they are detained, and upon which we propose to put them on trial. I refer to 5 Norris and Johnson 337, to illustrate what is conspiracy, rather than show that conspiracy to do an unlawful act is an indictable offense. The law punishes the conspiracy to prevent the unlawful act. The conspiracy constitutes the indictable offense, and that is sufficiently stated upon the face of the warrants. It is not necessary the conspiracy should be executed. The commitment as originally made out by the clerk, is very brief. It is a clerical misprison in not stating upon its face the cause of the commitment. This was discovered before the return, and the court ordered its correction. My friends ask for the authority of the court to amend its entries and correct the misprisions of a clerk. All courts of record have that power.

It is not to make a new charge, or to convert one charge into another, but to more distinctly charge the offense. I refer to 4 Johnson, 356. That was a case where a habeas corpus was issued to relieve a party from commitment for contempt. It was said the commitment was defective. If the attachment had been so defective as not to hold the party, the court could have issued a perfect commitment. If we were held to the first warrant, and that was defective, your Honor could quash it and order a proper warrant to be made out. That conspiracy contemplated a resort to brute force, and to the use of the *posse* of sheriff and the bayonets of the United States force. If that were made out, there would be probable cause for presuming a breach of the peace. It is sufficient to confine them upon the charge of contemplating a breach of the peace until they give bail to release themselves. If there were any doubt about the sufficiency of the first warrants there can be none in regard to the second warrants. I will concede that you have the power to put the party on trial before you for his guilt or innocence. Twenty other Judges of Maryland have the same power. Your determination against them carries us to Worcester, thence to Washington and to Somerset, and to all the other judges of Maryland, for a continual re-litigation of the case you try.

The extent to which you can be pressed is that the representative of the State shall show probable cause for its action. We have a paper which purports to be an order of removal by the Governor of Maryland, in the exercise of our unusual authority against the Police Commissioners of Baltimore: I admit the fact of such an order. It is served on Thursday ; on Friday commissions are given to Messrs. Young and Valiant. They take the prescribed oaths, and, full of these purposes, Mr. Valiant says, in answer to certain questons that they have resolved on Saturday morning to ask Messrs. Hindes and Wood to vacate their office. If they didn't do it they will turn them out by a *posse*. A *posse* is a body of men to exert force. Messrs. Hindes and Wood had 2,000 men, armed, at their backs, to support them. Against these the *posse* would not go unarmed, but armed to the teeth. If these are not sufficient, then they will call upon the army of the United States. That is an agreement between Young and Valiant to use force to turn these parties out of possession.

The declared purpose of both is that a *posse* is to be summoned to put them in forcible possession. Not finding the commissioners, they publish a proclamation, arrogating to themselves the power of police commissioners. That is an overt act. They authorize the sheriff to swear in two thousand men to assist them. They impose unlawful oaths upon these men. Are not these overt acts in furtherance of their conspiracy? You find the commissioners arrested. You find the sheriff arrested. Still, the officers of the Sheriff continue to swear in that *posse*, almost within view of the court. Is not that evidence of the sheriff's conspiracy. There was no evidence of actual riot, but there was an unlawful assemblage about his office, and they were being sworn in, in the execution of this conspiracy. A grand jury could indict him as a principal in this conspiracy. He was implicated in overt acts tending to accomplish the object of the conspiracy. That was sufficient grounds upon which the court could hold him under bonds to keep the peace. These warrants were the usual process looking to the ultimate action of the grand jury. But the commitment is final judgment, and no further action is to be taken until the party gives security to keep the peace.

Where is the case that will justify you in going behind those commitments in default of security to keep the peace? In the case of Maulsby, the commitment was until he produced certain papers. But the grand jury having expired, the function of the commitment was ended. You did not question the validity of the warrant at the time of the commitment. The commitment ought to be for life. If the party is contumacious, and will not obey the order, he ought to be retained in confinement. Upon all the analogies of the case —a refusal to give bail to keep the peace—the commitment is in the nature of final execution. The party would be relieved at the next term of the court, if the grand jury did not act in the case. Can we not go behind the great seal of the State? If a successor was appointed by the Governor to Judge Martin, we could go behind the great seal and show it was improperly used by him. We could show that he had no authority, or that he had improperly exercised this authority. Our friends want us to admit that a proper case was raised before the Governor, that he had the proper authority, that he had properly exercised his authority, and then, upon their theory, we are to argue the Constitutional question. Such a question cannot be determined by your Honor in this summary proceedings. That question is out of the way. If he had the power to remove us, and rightfully exercised that power, and all these facts were proved before you, it would be no answer to the charge against these parties—that they were conspiring to enforce their right in an unlawful manner. Can parties claiming to freehold of which I am possessed, conspire to thrust me out by force? Then close all courts of justice If they had title, they had no right to conspire with the sheriff, and secure his posse, and the army of the United States, and the militia of the neighboring States lately in rebellion, to use such force in depriving us of our franchises. What is the evidence of title ! A copy of the sentence taken from a letter press. I will not take advantage of this point. I have seen the original with the great seal of the State affixed. Is the sentence alone evidence of title, without a copy of the charges or of the testimony in the case ! I should like to see a case to this point. The Governor says he has discharged these people for official misconduct, but the memorial not being here, you don't know what the charges are. The Governor is of inferior jurisdiction, and is subject to all the restraints of a specially delegated jurisdiction. It is, therefore, not sufficient to place upon the order the simple fact of the sentence, but all the facts must be exhibited which led to that judgment. I refer to 2 Burroughs, 731. It is true that where an emotion is returned all the necessary facts must be exhibited to show that the emotion was in proper and legal form. The court must say whether the facts found by the Governor were cause of removal. That is rule applicable to the exercises of special authority. Cases are in the books where the facts were set out, and the courts decided they were not cause for removal. These gentlemen never attempted to put themselves rightfully in possession of this office. Mr. Young was appointed in place of Mr. Hindes, and Mr. Valiant in place of Mr. Wood. Each could only claim a seat at the board. They did not go there and respectively claim a seat at the board. That Board is composed of three persons. They never put themselves in communication with the Mayor. They never summoned him to attend their meeting. They open a distinct office and arrogate to themselves conjointly the functions and authority of the

Board of Police. I think I have shown sufficient cause why
this writ of habas corpus should be quashed, and I will not
dwell upon this point.

ARGUMENT OF MR. SCHLEY.

Mr. Schley, Esq., said, "before I proceed to discuss the
respective cases now under examination, I propose very brief-
ly to discuss the duties and powers of local judges in respect
to the writ of habas corpus. It is perfectly unimportant to
consider what were the duties of judges in England in early
times : which have been so elaborately discussed on the other
side. It was the duty of your Honor to grant the writs in
the cases before you, otherwise you would have been liable in
a penalty of $500, at suit of the parties making application.
The parties are before you, and we are to consider what *now* are
your duties, and powers under the law. Mr. Schley then
read the state law of Maryland on the subject, which requires
that a judge shall immediately inquire into the cause of the
caption and detention of the parties imprisoned, and that he
shall discharge them upon insufficient cause. Also, that a
party many controvert the return, or plead any matter, and
summon witnesses to testify in relation to it. The argument
on the other side, although, under the law, you may hear the
evidence of witnesses, that their testimony is to be disregarded, and you must remand the prisoners into custody.

Is that the meaning of the law ? That you cannot go behind the return to show that the charges are false. Such a
narrow construction of the law was never designed and never
claimed. If this could be done, the writ of habeas corpus
would be undeserving of the eulogies which have ever been
pronounced upon it as the safeguard of every citizen to his
freedom and liberty.

Mr. Schley hoped that political feeling or bias will never
enter into any court or influence its decision. He would retire from practice in any case where he had reason to believe
that political feeling would bias the result.

The Governor's opinion of his power to remove the Police
Commissioners is concurred in almost unanimously by the
legal profession and by a large preponderance of the voters
of the city.

He next referred to the case of Sheriff Thompson. The
Judge of the Criminal Court had no right to issue the
warrant for his arrest without oath or affirmation except
upon view. Did Judge Bond act upon view ? Could he see
through the walls of the court house ? It is absurd to say
he acted "upon view." The grand jury were in session, and
could have indicted the parties had there been *ex parte* testimony to justify their action.

Every man, before commitment, must hear the charges

against him and be confronted by his witnesses, but we are told that these gentlemen have been convicted of riot, and committed to jail, without the intervention of the grand jury. This differs with other cases. Persons were summoned by the Sheriff to be sworn in as a *posse comitatus*, and it cannot be an unlawful assemblage when they come there to obey the law.

Mr. Schley then reviewed the law defining what constituted a rout and riot. There must be something to cause terror and consternation and a tumultuous assemblage, to constitute a riot. There was no evidence that there were any such proceedings at the Sheriff's office. In the case of Mr. Young, he was arrested without oath or warrant. He was arrested upon the evidence of Fuller, which related only to Mr. Valiant. What Mr. Valiant said to Fuller did not implicate Mr. Young, although Fuller said Mr. Valiant used the word "we." The concert of action between the two must be shown before the statement of one can be given in evidence against the other. The demand made by them does not imply that they intended to take any but legal measures to obtain their office.

Judge Bartol said—My inquiry is simply as a magistrate to determine the question of probable cause. The Commissioners have issued a proclamation addressed to the police force, which paper was not objected to.

Mr. Schley.—There was nothing in the paper to show that the Commissioners did not proceed by mandamus. I do not think that the Governor authorized them to take the office by the *posse comitatus*. I hope that when your honor decides this case, as I trust you will in favor of the new appointees, that the ex-Commissioners will gracefully retire from office. I hope that there will be good and true men surrounding them, who will so advise them, and that in an hour afterwards, they will come forward and say, "We surrender the office." I look forward with a strong hope, now that the election is over, that they will yield up the office, without the necessity of a *mandamus* or a *quo warranto*. There was no evidence to authorize the arrest of Mr. Young. He and the Sheriff were arrested without law, upon no oath or affirmation, and I rely upon the same principles of civil liberty in both cases.

Mr. Schley then reviewed the proceedings under which the Commissioners were arrested, and asked, "Is there no limitation upon the power of a court to commit a man for one offence and try him for another?" The opposite counsel say the commitment used on Saturday to keep the peace is finality. But on Monday an amended order of commitment is issued, charging them with conspiracy. One commitment requires them to keep the peace by desisting from any attempt to exercise the duties of their office. That is one of the most extraordinary documents on record. If it had been prepared with a design, it could not have been more artfully, or I should say, skillfully framed. If they had given bond under it, they would have been precluded by its terms from ever attempting to obtain the office, even by mandamus, and would have forfeited their recognizance by so doing. The other party would have forever remained *de facto* Commissioners. Had the Commissioners a right to barter away the rights of the people?—to abandon the duties and control of the funds of the city to others in order to obtain their personal liberty?

Suppose the General Assembly instead of the Governor had removed the Commissioners, it is asserted that the new appointees would have to come into court to obtain their office by mandamus. Is the authority of the General Assembly to be set at nought and defied in this way? Suppose a judge is removed from office by the Legislature, is he to be allowed to go on administering the law as a *de facto* judge? The Governor in this case has the same power as the General Assembly, and his acts have the same force as the acts of the Legislature.

Mr. Schley then referred to a case in which the Pope had issued a sentence of excommunication, in which the question arose whether the act of his Holiness went into effect *eo instante*, or took effect after notice. In this case, said Mr. Schley, we took care to give the notice. He then referred to the case of Ford, in which the Clerk of the Court amended the verdict of the jury, which the Court of Appeals set aside as an illegal act. He denied that the Judge of the Criminal Court had any power to amend the charge and commitment in the absence of the accused. The second commitment is a nullity until the first is got rid of. He was informed that it had been the practice of the Criminal Court to amend commitments in that way, but it is a bad practice, and ought to be abolished.

The great question in this cause is, are the newly appointed Commissioners, the Police Commissioners. He would not argue before the court as to the power of the Governor to remove and appoint Commissioners. Suppose complaint had been made to the General Assembly, and that body had made the removal, would its power have been denied? If the old Commissioners will not give up, they are assuming a great personal responsibility. Their acts are illegal, and they can be made liable in damages for what they do. We need no mandamus—the seal of the Governor is sufficient. The Judge of the Criminal Court seeks to stay the execution of law and decide the question of title. "Upon what meat does this our Cæsar feed that he has grown so great?" The validity of his action involves the question of title, and it becomes the duty of your Honor to pronounce the decision of that question.

We and the country will be gratified to have your decision on that point. The settlement of this question would restore the State to that condition of peace and quietness which once existed, and to which all of its citizens have been looking forward with fond hopes and expectations. God grant that it may soon arrive. The Maryland of to-day is not the Maryland of his youth. May our beloved State become what it has been in the past, the home of chivalric citizens and of women, beautiful and pure, the latter uncontaminated by politics, and removed from its debasing influences. He wished never to see a woman with a political newspaper in her hand. Our beloved State, freed from the unhappy excitements of politics, may go in the prosperous career which awaits the efforts of its people.

Mr. Schley's remarks upon this subject, or rather his beautiful apostrophe to the spirit of liberty, concord and social harmony, was uttered with a degree of enthusiasm and eloquence that he said he felt called upon to excuse himself to his Honor for having been ,in the excitement of the moment, led into observations perhaps foreign to the subject of his argument.

REMARKS OF MR. RODGERS.

Mr. Rodgers said he had been requested by the State's Attorney to request his Honor, in rendering his opinion in this case, to state the grounds upon which his decision is based, so that he could be governed thereby in any future action which he might be required to take. He said, if these gentlemen are discharged, and they should assume to act as before their commitments, and which action the State's Attorney thought was ground for their arrest, and which no doubt would lead to a breach of the peace, he would again be compelled to renew the application to the Criminal Court, to place them again under arrest. The law of habeas corpus, he knew, would not allow a party, when discharged, to be arrested again for the same offence, and therefore they wanted to have grounds upon which the decision of the Court was based, accurately based.

Mr. Latrobe.—You had better wait until the decision is rendered, then you can take measures for your action. Sufficient for the day is the evil thereof.

Orville Horwitz, Esq., said it would be equally gratifying to the counsel for petitioners if his Honor would, in his written opinion, state the grounds of his decision.

Judge Bartol said, in view of the magnitude of the interests involved in the case, he would take time to carefully consider his opinion, and would give it in writing on Tuesday next, at 12 o'clock, in the Superior Court room.

11

With the assent of the counsel and the State, the petitioners were allowed to remain at liberty, upon the assurance that they would be present on Tuesday to abide the decision of Judge Bartol.

TUESDAY MORNING, NOV. 13.

Precisely at 12 o'clock, Judge Bartol proceeded to read his opinion, for which see page 8.

REMARKS OF COUNSEL.

. Upon the conclusion of the reading of the decision, J. H. B. Latrobe, Esq., counsel for petitioners, addressed the Judge as follows:

It is proper I should say that the proceeding by mandamus on the part of the Police Commissioners, Young and Valiant, whom you have adjudged to be entitled to the franchise of their office, in order to obtain possession of the property and effects thereto belonging, was that which their counsel had advised them to pursue from the beginning, and the Commissioners and their counsel alike regret that the remarks made by Mr. Valiant, as proved by Messrs. Fuller and Ball, and referred to by your Honor, and which I am authorized by Mr. Valiant to say were his own exclusively, and made without the knowledge of Mr. Young, should have rendered it necessary in your Honor's judgment to hold the Commissioners to bail on the charge of conspiracy to do that by the strong arm which a more peaceful remedy would have lawfully effected. Even had your Honor's opinion in this connection not been expressed, a mandamus would have been resorted to, as it will now be resorted to, if necessary, to obtain the property and effects belonging to the Board of Police. The Commissioners will at once give their recognizance in the sum prescribed.

Thos. S. Alexander, counsel for respondents, then addressed the Judge as follows:

The counsel for the Commissioners of the Board of Police ask permission to state that they advised the Commissioners that the Governor had not rightfully removed them from their office of Commissioners, and it was in consequence of this advice that the Commissioners resolved to retain office until the question of title was properly determined on mandamus. They state, further, that on being informed of the declarations made by Mr. Valiant, which were proven by Messrs. Fuller and Ball, they advised the Commissioners that such declarations were evidence of conspiracy, for which Messrs. Valiant and Young might be held to answer before the Criminal Court of Baltimore city, and that it was the duty of the said Commissioners to lay the evidence of such declarations before the State's Attorney for the city, in order that he should take such action thereon as he might think necessary for maintaining the peace of the city,

Mr. Latrobe prepared the orders for the release of the Commissioners, Messrs. Young and Valiant. The order in the case of Mr. Valiant is given ; that of Mr. Young being similar.

In the matter of the petition of Wm. T. Valiant for habeas corpus, Judge Bartol, of the Court of Appeals of Maryland:

Ordered, this 13th day of November, in the year 1866, that the petitioner be discharged from the custody of the Warden of the Jail of Baltimore city, on the commitment in default of bail in the sum of $5,000, and that he be discharged from the same custody, under the commitment on the order requiring bail in the sum of $20,000, upon this giving his own recognizance in the sum of $5,000, conditioned for his appearance before the Criminal Court of Baltimore City to answer the charge of conspiracy therein depending against him.

[Seal.]   JAMES L. BARTOL,
Judge of the Court of Appeals of Maryland.

The bond required by the above order has been given.
November 14th, 1866.   JAMES L. BARTOL.

The bond given by the Commissioners in their own recognizance, upon the charge of conspiracy, to answer before the Criminal Court, reads thus :

"Know all men by these presents, that I, James Young, am held and firmly buond unto the State of Maryland in the sum of five thousand dollars, to be paid to the said State or to its certain attorney, to which payment, well and truly to be made and done, I bind myself, my heirs, executors and administrators firmly by these presents. Sealed with my seal, dated the 13th day of November, 1866.

"The condition of the above obligation is such, that if the said James Young shall well and truly appear before the Criminal Court of Baltimore city, to answer the charge of conspiracy therein depending against him, shall be void and of non-effect.

[Seal.]   JAMES YOUNG.

"Signed, sealed and delivered in presence of James Bartol."

The bond given by Mr. Valiant is in the precise words of the above. Both bonds have been filed in the office of the Criminal Court.

www.ingramcontent.com/pod-product-compliance
Lightning Source LLC
Chambersburg PA
CBHW020326090426

42735CB00009B/1421